PHYSICIANS

THIRD EDITION

Careers in Focus

PHYSICIANS

THIRD EDITION

Ferguson
An imprint of Infobase Publishing

Careers in Focus: Physicians, Third Edition

Ferguson
An imprint of Infobase Publishing
132 West 31st Street
New York NY 10001

Library of Congress Cataloging-in-Publication Data
Careers in focus. Physicians. — 3rd ed.
     p. cm.
   Includes bibliographical references and index.
   ISBN-13: 978-0-8160-8027-4 (hardcover : alk. paper)
   ISBN-10: 0-8160-8027-5 (hardcover : alk. paper) 1. Medicine—Vocational guidance—Juvenile literature. 2. Physicians—Juvenile literature. I. Ferguson Publishing. II. Title: Physicians.
   R690.C38 2010
   610.69—dc22   2010028399

Ferguson books are available at special discounts when purchased in bulk quantities for businesses, associations, institutions, or sales promotions. Please call our Special Sales Department in New York at (212) 967-8800 or (800) 322-8755.

You can find Ferguson on the World Wide Web at
http://www.infobasepublishing.com

Text design by David Strelecky
Composition by Lina Farinella
Cover printed by Yurchak Printing, Landisville, Pa.
Book printed and bound by Yurchak Printing, Landisville, Pa.
Printed in the United States of America

This book is printed on acid-free paper.

All links and Web addresses were checked and verified to be correct at the time of publication. Because of the dynamic nature of the Web, some addresses and links may have changed since publication and may no longer be valid.

Table of Contents

Introduction

The single most familiar career in the medical industry is that of the physician. For many years, the main health consultant was the family physician. General practitioners still serve the role of the family doctor to many families in the United States, but the role and the medical care delivery of the family doctor have changed.

According to the U.S. Department of Labor, the majority of doctors in the United States are specialists. General practitioners will handle most medical problems, but when an emergency or problem arises that the family doctor may not have the equipment or capability to handle, the patient is referred to a specialist. The patient may rely on his or her generalist to recommend a specialist, or the patient may be able to determine which type of specialist is needed. For skin problems, for example, most patients would know to consult with a dermatologist.

Internists, who account for about 15 percent of all physicians in the United States, are frequently used as general practitioners. They are capable of handling most medical concerns and will make referrals to specialists as needed. There are 36 different general medical care specialties for the physician to choose from while in medical school (ranging from anesthesiology to urology) and many more subspecialties. About one-quarter of practicing physicians specialize in some aspect of surgery. The rest work in one specific area of the body, one specific element of treatment, or with specific clientele. For example, pediatricians work with children; neurologists work with problems of the nervous system; psychiatrists diagnose and treat emotional, mental, and behavioral disorders; and anesthesiologists handle anesthetization during surgical procedures.

Earnings for physicians are among the highest in any occupation. Physicians also spend the longest time preparing for their career, and their education is expensive. All physicians must earn a bachelor's degree and then apply to medical school. Four years of medical school leads to an M.D. (doctor of medicine) or D.O. (doctor of osteopathy) degree. Students then must pass an exam that certifies them to practice medicine. They then complete a one- to two-year internship. The internship is followed by a residency, which takes from one to seven years to complete, depending on the specialty. Subspecialties (for example, vascular surgery is a subspecialty of surgery) require additional training (usually called a fellowship) that can take one to three years. The training is long and intense, but the rewards are great, both in terms of job satisfaction and financial compensation.

According to the U.S. Department of Labor, the health care industry will be the fastest growing segment of the job market through 2018, accounting for 22 percent of all new wage and salary jobs during that time period. Employment for physicians is predicted to grow much faster than the average for all occupations during that time period. As the nation's elderly population continues to grow, the demand for well-trained general practitioners and specialists of all varieties will be great. In addition, specialists will be in demand in rural and low-income areas where the quality of health care is poor and physicians are scarce. Many new physicians will find work in group practices, clinics, and health networks. As more people begin to investigate the benefits of complementary and alternative medicine and therapies, physicians with specializations in areas such as Ayurvedic medicine and homeopathy will find their services are in demand in the coming years, as well.

Each article in *Careers in Focus: Physicians* discusses a particular physician occupation in detail. The articles appear in Ferguson's *Encyclopedia of Careers and Vocational Guidance*, but they have been updated and revised with the latest information from the U.S. Department of Labor, professional organizations, and other sources. The following paragraphs detail the sections and features that appear in the book.

The **Quick Facts** section provides a brief summary of the career, including recommended school subjects, personal skills, work environment, minimum educational requirements, salary ranges, certification or licensing requirements, and employment outlook. This section also provides acronyms and identification numbers for the following government classification indexes: the Dictionary of Occupational Titles (DOT), the Guide for Occupational Exploration (GOE), the National Occupational Classification (NOC) Index, and the Occupational Information Network (O*NET)-Standard Occupational Classification System (SOC) index. The DOT, GOE, and O*NET-SOC indexes have been created by the U.S. government; the NOC index is Canada's career classification system. Readers can use the identification numbers listed in the Quick Facts section to access further information about a career. Print editions of the DOT (*Dictionary of Occupational Titles.* Indianapolis, Ind.: JIST Works, 1991) and GOE (*Guide for Occupational Exploration.* Indianapolis, Ind.: JIST Works, 2001) are available at libraries. Electronic versions of the NOC (http://www23.hrdc-drhc.gc.ca) and O*NET-SOC (http://online.onetcenter.org) are available on the Internet. When no DOT, GOE, NOC, or O*NET-SOC numbers are listed, this means that the U.S. Department of Labor or Human Resources and Skills Development Canada have not created a numerical designation for this career. In this instance, you will see the acronym "N/A," or not available.

The **Overview** section is a brief introductory description of the duties and responsibilities involved in this career. Oftentimes, a career may have a variety of job titles. When this is the case, alternative career titles are presented. Employment statistics are also provided, when available. The **History** section describes the history of the particular job as it relates to the overall development of its industry or field. **The Job** describes the primary and secondary duties of the job. **Requirements** discusses high school and postsecondary education and training requirements, any certification or licensing that is necessary, and other personal requirements for success in the job. **Exploring** offers suggestions on how to gain experience in or knowledge of the particular job before making a firm educational and financial commitment. The focus is on what can be done while still in high school (or in the early years of college) to gain a better understanding of the job. The **Employers** section gives an overview of typical places of employment for the job. **Starting Out** discusses the best ways to land that first job, be it through the college career services office, newspaper ads, Internet employment sites, or personal contact. The **Advancement** section describes what kind of career path to expect from the job and how to get there. **Earnings** lists salary ranges and describes the typical fringe benefits. The **Work Environment** section describes the typical surroundings and conditions of employment—whether indoors or outdoors, noisy or quiet, social or independent. Also discussed are typical hours worked, any seasonal fluctuations, and the stresses and strains of the job. The **Outlook** section summarizes the job in terms of the general economy and industry projections. For the most part, Outlook information is obtained from the U.S. Bureau of Labor Statistics and is supplemented by information gathered from professional associations. Job growth terms follow those used in the *Occupational Outlook Handbook*. Growth described as "much faster than the average" means an increase of 21 percent or more. Growth described as "faster than the average" means an increase of 14 to 20 percent. Growth described as "about as fast as the average" means an increase of 7 to 13 percent. Growth described as "more slowly than the average" means an increase of 3 to 6 percent. "Little or no change" means a decrease of 2 percent to an increase of 2 percent. "Decline" means a decrease of 3 percent or more. Each article ends with **For More Information**, which lists organizations that provide information on training, education, internships, scholarships, and job placement.

Careers in Focus: Physicians also includes photos, informative sidebars, and interviews with professionals in the field.

*You will see that some of the sections described are missing from some of the physician specialty articles. That is because the information in those sections is the same as in the articles "Physicians" or "Osteopaths." If you are interested in a physician specialty, it is suggested that you read the "Physicians" and/or "Osteopaths" articles first, since all specialists must first become physicians (either specializing in allopathic or osteopathic medicine).

Allergists/ Immunologists

OVERVIEW

Allergists/immunologists are physicians who specialize in the treatment of allergic, asthmatic, and immunologic diseases. They treat patients with asthma, hay fever, food allergies, AIDS, allergic diseases of the eye and skin, rheumatoid arthritis, and other diseases. There are more than 5,900 board-certified allergists/immunologists employed in the United States.

HISTORY

The first great physician was Hippocrates, a Greek who lived almost 2,500 years ago. He developed theories about the practice of medicine and the anatomy of the human body, but Hippocrates is remembered today for a set of medical ethics that continues to influence medical practice. The oath that he administered to his disciples is still administered to physicians about to start practice. His 87 treatises on medicine, known as the Hippocratic Collection, are believed to be the first authoritative record of early medical theory and practice. Hippocratic physicians believed in the theory that health was maintained by a proper balance of four "humors" in the body: blood, phlegm, black bile, and yellow bile.

Since the time of Ancient Greece, as you might imagine, there have been many advances in the medical field: the development of organized clinical instruction, vaccinations, sterilization procedures, and instruments such as the stethoscope, to

What Is Today's Pollen Count?

Tree, grass, and weed pollen and mold spores are some of the most common causes of seasonal allergies (hay fever). Allergy symptoms are at their worst when the counts of these substances in the air are at their highest—typically in spring and fall.

The National Allergy Bureau, a division of the American Academy of Allergy, Asthma, and Immunology, sponsors a Web site that tracks daily levels of tree, weed, and grass pollen and mold spores in approximately 78 areas of the United States. Monitoring these trends helps physicians and allergy sufferers stay informed about the severity of the current allergy season. Visit http://www.aaaai.org/nab and click on the link for "Pollen Levels" to see what the allergy forecast is for your neighborhood.

name a few. In addition to these advances, the medical profession also saw the development of specialists, doctors who concentrate their work in specific areas such as surgery, psychiatry, internal medicine, or allergies and immunology.

THE JOB

More than 54 percent of Americans suffer from some kind of allergy. Allergies to certain foods, plants, pollen, animal fur, air pollution, insects, colognes, chemicals, and cleansers may send sufferers to *allergy and immunology specialists,* doctors who specialize in the treatment of allergic, asthmatic, and immunologic diseases.

Allergists and immunologists also treat patients with hay fever, also called allergic rhinitis, which causes symptoms such as congestion, sneezing, and a scratchy throat brought on by pollens or molds in the air. They treat asthma, a respiratory disease often triggered by an allergic reaction that causes restricted breathing, constricting the airflow to the lungs. Another serious allergic reaction is anaphylaxis. Triggered by a particular food or insect sting, anaphylaxis can quickly restrict breathing, swell the throat, and cause unconsciousness. Other allergies treated by an allergist include skin allergies, such as hives and eczema, and food and drug allergies.

Immunologic diseases are those that affect the immune system. Allergy and immunology specialists treat patients with conditions such as AIDS, rheumatoid arthritis, and lupus. An immunologist also treats patients who are receiving an organ or bone marrow transplant to help prevent the patient's body from rejecting the transplanted organ.

Allergists/immunologists first examine patients. They review medical histories and backgrounds and may also conduct skin tests and blood tests. Skin tests are often preferred because they are inexpensive and the results are available immediately. Skin tests are also better for identifying more subtle allergies.

Once the diagnosis is made, the doctor determines a treatment plan. In some cases, the solution may be as simple as avoiding the things that cause the allergic reaction. The allergist suggests ways to limit patients' exposure to the allergen. In other cases, a doctor prescribes medication such as antihistamines to relieve allergy symptoms such as nasal congestion, eye burning, and skin rashes.

Antihistamines can have side effects such as dizziness, headaches, and nausea. Should these side effects occur, the allergist may lower a dosage or prescribe a different medication. Sometimes a patient can build up a resistance to an antihistamine, and the doctor needs to prescribe a stronger variety.

Immunotherapy (a series of allergy shots) is another kind of treatment for asthma and for allergies to pollen, dust, bee venom, and a variety of other substances. Immunotherapy involves injecting the patient with a small amount of the substance that causes the allergic reaction. The immune system then becomes less sensitive to the substances and reduces the symptoms of allergy. An allergist will give weekly shots over an extended time, gradually increasing the dosage; eventually the shots are only necessary once a month.

REQUIREMENTS

High School
If you are interested in becoming an allergist/immunologist, start preparing for this career in high school by taking college preparatory classes. Science classes, including biology, chemistry, and physics are especially important. Math and English classes will help you develop skills working with numbers and research. Social science classes can give you a better understanding of people and society.

Postsecondary Training
After earning an M.D. or D.O. degree and becoming licensed to practice medicine (see "Physicians" and "Osteopathic Physicians"), allergists/immunologists must complete a three-year residency in internal medicine or pediatrics, then a minimum of two years of training in an allergy and immunology fellowship. The American

Academy of Allergy, Asthma, and Immunology publishes a training program directory, which lists accredited training programs and faculty and program information.

Certification or Licensing
Certification from the American Board of Allergy and Immunology requires a valid medical license, proof of residency completion, and written evaluation from the residency director. The evaluation reviews the candidate's clinical judgment, attitude, professional behavior, and other work skills and habits. The certification exam tests the candidate's knowledge of the immune system, human pathology, and the molecular basis of allergic and other immune reactions. The candidate must also show an understanding of diagnostic tests and therapy for immunologic diseases. Dual certification is also available in allergy/immunology and pediatric pulmonology, adult rheumatology, and pediatric rheumatology. There are more than 5,900 certified allergists/immunologists in the United States.

All physicians in the United States must be licensed to practice. Some states have reciprocity agreements with other states so that a physician licensed in one state may be automatically licensed in another without being required to pass another examination.

Other Requirements
Allergists/immunologists should be compassionate and concerned for the well-being of their patients. They should also be careful listeners—a doctor must have a good understanding of a patient's background, environment, and emotional state to plan the best treatment. An allergist/immunologist must be prepared to deal with the stress of caring for sick patients; some of these patients may have life-threatening diseases such as AIDS, cancer, or severe asthma.

EARNINGS
Physicians are rewarded well for their years of intensive study, for their long hours, and for their level of responsibility. The median annual income for all physicians in 2009, according to the U.S. Department of Labor, was about $186,044 per year. Salaries for physicians who specialize in internal medicine ranged from $175,200 to $209,845, according to *Modern Healthcare*'s 2008 Physician Compensation Survey. A number of factors, such as geographical location, experience, and reputation of good work, can determine an allergist/immunologist's salary. First-year medical interns earned $47,458 in 2009, according to the Association of American Medical Colleges.

Benefits for allergists/immunologists include vacation and sick time, health, and sometimes dental, insurance, and pension or 401(k) plans. Allergists/immunologists who have their own practices must provide their own benefits.

OUTLOOK

Employment of physicians will grow much faster than the average for all careers through 2018, according to the U.S. Department of Labor. As many as 40 to 50 million Americans suffer from some kind of allergy, fueling the demand for allergists/immunologists. Though some doctors remain skeptical about the relationship between allergy and illness, allergy/immunology has become a respected field of medicine. As this field continues to grow, more doctors will refer their patients to these specialists.

FOR MORE INFORMATION

For career information and a list of accredited training programs, contact
American Academy of Allergy, Asthma, and Immunology
555 East Wells Street, Suite 1100
Milwaukee, WI 53202-3823
Tel: 414-272-6071
E-mail: info@aaaai.org
http://www.aaaai.org

For information on immunology, such as research, graduate programs, and fellowships, contact
American Association of Immunologists
9650 Rockville Pike
Bethesda, MD 20814-3999
Tel: 301-634-7178
E-mail: infoaai@aai.org
http://www.aai.org

For information on certification, contact
American Board of Allergy and Immunology
111 South Independence Mall East, Suite 701
Philadelphia, PA 19106-2512
Tel: 866-264-5568
E-mail: abai@abai.org
http://www.abai.org

INTERVIEW

Dr. Michael Pistiner is an allergist/immunologist in Leominster, Massachusetts, and a clinical instructor at Children's Hospital Boston, Harvard Medical School. He discussed his career with the editors of Careers in Focus: Physicians.

Q. What made you want to become an allergist?

A. While I was in the eighth grade I decided that I wanted to be a pediatrician. As life would have it, I realized this dream and completed my four years of medical school, then entered a pediatric residency program. It was as an intern, a first-year pediatric resident, that I took care of one particular child with a rare primary immunodeficiency. I took care of him from the time that he initially became sick with recurrent and rare infections until after he was given a specific diagnosis and managed for his immunodeficiency. I found these types of disorders fascinating and caring for children with them imperative and critical. The early and accurate diagnosis and management of a child with immunodeficiency can be life saving. Once I realized my newfound interest, knowing that training as an immunologist is coupled with training as an allergist, I began focusing my efforts on learning more about allergic disorders. I found that this was equally fascinating and incredibly fulfilling, although in a slightly different way. I was taken by the fact that many of the allergic disorders, if diagnosed appropriately, are so treatable. Many people with allergic disease can achieve great health and, unlike many other fields, cures are achievable.

Q. What's a typical day like on the job for you?

A. Allergist/immunologists have very different job descriptions depending on their interests. To apply to fellowship programs, M.D.s or D.O.s either first complete a three-year pediatric or internal medicine residency program. Fellowship programs range from two to three additional years of training. All include clinical training, with differing emphasis in each program on research, types of disorders, and differing patient populations. Once training is complete an allergist/immunologist can pursue many different jobs. One can choose to remain in academic medicine, where he or she can have a clinical role, a research role, or some mixture of the above. Additionally, some can primarily focus on allergy, while others may focus on immunology/immunodeficiency, and many, a mixture of the above. Many graduating fellows pursue jobs in private practice, where the majority of care is devoted to clinical allergy. There is a wide range in practice size and hours worked.

I have been fortunate in finding a mixture of academic and private practice that works well for me and my interests. I work in private practice, where I care for both children and adults. Although the majority of what I manage are allergic disorders, including asthma, food allergy, allergic rhinitis, hives, eczema, stinging insect allergy, and drug allergies, I do see immunodeficiency from time to time. I work from about 7:45 A.M. to 5:00 P.M. Additionally, I volunteer at Children's Hospital Boston working on research that focuses on teaching coping skills to children with food allergies and their parents. I have been out of training now for about one-and-a-half years and am very happy with my career choice. I feel that the field of allergy/immunology (A/I) offers the unique ability to individualize career opportunities.

Q. What are some of the pros and cons of your job?

A. As there are a variety of options once in the field of A/I it is relatively easy to individualize what it is that you do. This field offers the ability to pursue specific interests. Another plus, especially in private practice, is that there is a need for allergists in most geographic areas. We are not limited to only major cities. Geography, though, can become limiting with more narrow interests (e.g., primary immunodeficiency, pediatric food allergy, basic immunology, etc.). Allergists/immunologists have not been immune to the current downturn of the economy. Many have noted decreased numbers of patients as economic burden has caused many to hold off on seeking health care.

Q. What are the most important personal and professional qualities for allergists/immunologists?

A. Versatility is a major plus. As there are so many different career options, there are so many different attributes that make one well suited for each path. For example, those with an inclination toward lab work and basic immunology would be well suited for basic immunology research. Those who enjoy patient contact and clinical work may make good clinicians. Much of the management of allergic and immunologic disorders does require one to be detail oriented.

Q. What is the future employment outlook for allergists/immunologists?

A. The future employment outlook for allergists is excellent. A recent Center for Health Workforce Study notes that while allergies and asthma are on the rise, the supply of allergists is decreasing and may fall below demand in the near future.

Anesthesiologists

OVERVIEW

Anesthesiologists are physicians who specialize in the planning, performance, and maintenance of a patient's anesthesia during surgical, obstetric, or other medical procedures. Using special equipment, monitors, and drugs, the anesthesiologist makes sure the patient feels no pain and remains uninjured during the procedure. There are more than 37,450 anesthesiologists employed in the United States.

HISTORY

Before the mid-19th century, when modern anesthetics started to be developed, you would most likely live with your affliction or undergo surgery with little or no help for pain. Often patients would need to be restrained. An 18th-century French encyclopedia described how to perform bladder surgery by first restraining the patient in a special "surgical chair."

Efforts to manage pain have been a constant in human history. A variety of substances and techniques have been used, including opium, cannabis, alcohol, mandragora root, and hypnotism. None of these proved entirely reliable or completely effective.

Nitrous oxide, developed in the late 18th century, was the first gas recognized to have anesthetic properties. Its effects, which included giddiness, earned it the nickname of "laughing gas." Ether was developed shortly after nitrous oxide. Neither gas, however, was used to anesthetize humans at that time. In fact, nitrous oxide was often used for entertainment purposes at "laughing gas parties" or by sideshow entertainers.

The first successful use of ether as an anesthetic occurred in 1842 when Dr. Crawford W. Long used it when he removed a tumor from a friend's neck. Dr. Long, however, failed to publicize the event, and in 1846 a Boston dentist, Dr. William T. G. Morton, became credited with the discovery of general anesthesia when he successfully administered ether to anesthetize a patient while removing a tumor. As one would imagine, ether's reputation spread quickly. So did the reputation of chloroform, used successfully for the first time in 1847.

Anesthesiology continued to advance, and in 1875 intravenous administration of anesthetics was developed. Greater study of anesthesiology in the 20th and 21st centuries has led to many advances, and anesthesiology has become increasingly more sophisticated, revolutionizing the practice of surgery.

THE JOB

Anesthesiologists make sure that the patient's body is not overstimulated or injured by a medical procedure and that the patient feels no pain while undergoing the procedure. Traditionally, anesthesiologists deal mainly in the area of surgery. They do, however, also oversee the administration of anesthetics during other medical procedures, and if needed, during childbirth.

Questions to Ask

Surgery and anesthesiology are daunting prospects for most people. However, learning as much as you can about the surgical procedure and anesthetics you will be receiving may help to demystify the experience for you and lessen any fears you may have.

The American Society of Anesthesiologists recommends asking your anesthesiologist the following questions before surgery:

- What are the anesthesiologist's qualifications? How many procedures has he or she performed?
- Who else will be involved in my anesthesia care?
- Will I meet with an anesthesiologist before surgery?
- What do you monitor besides my heart and breathing?
- Do you have a 24-hour recovery room? If not, where will I recover?
- Who will manage my pain-control needs after surgery?

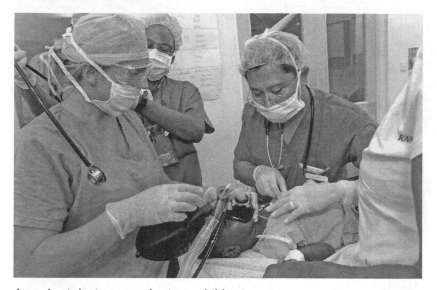

Anesthesiologists anesthetize a child prior to surgery. *(Chet Gordon, The Image Works)*

After reviewing a patient's medical history, the anesthesiologist will determine the best form of anesthesia for the patient. Different medical problems and various kinds of surgery require different kinds of anesthesia. These determinations are based on the anesthesiologist's broad background in medicine, which includes an understanding of surgical procedures, physiology, pharmacology, and critical care.

In the operating room, an anesthesiologist gives the patient an anesthetic, making the patient unconscious and numb to pain. This involves administering drugs to put the patient under and maintaining the anesthesia. In some cases, only a regional anesthesia is required—numbing only the part of the body on which the surgery is being performed. In more complex cases, anesthesiologists may need to prepare special equipment such as blood-warming devices. Anesthesiologists use monitoring equipment and insert intravenous lines and breathing tubes. They make sure the gas mask is secure and allows for a proper airway. In an emergency situation, an anesthesiologist is also part of the cardiopulmonary resuscitation team.

An anesthesiologist pays close attention to the patient's well-being by monitoring blood pressure, breathing, heart rate, and body temperature throughout surgery. It is also the anesthesiologist's responsibility to position the patient properly, so that the doctor can perform the surgery and the patient remains uninjured. The anesthesiologist also controls the patient's temperature, cooling or heating different parts of the body during surgery.

Anesthesiologists are not limited to the operating room; they also spend time with patients before and after surgery. When meeting the patient beforehand, an anesthesiologist explains the kind of anesthesia to be used and answers any questions. This interaction helps put the patient at ease and allows the anesthesiologist to get to know the patient before surgery. Unlike other doctors, anesthesiologists do not have the opportunity to work closely for long periods of time with patients.

Anesthesiologists may specialize in different areas, such as pediatric anesthesia, respiratory therapy, critical care, and cardiovascular anesthesia. They often work in teams, consisting of anesthesiology residents, nurse anesthetists, and anesthesiology assistants. The anesthesiologist will delegate responsibilities to other members of the care team.

While emergency cases require anesthesiologists to make quick decisions and act without hesitation, in other cases they have time to carefully plan, to study a patient's medical history, to meet with the surgeons and the patients, and to work by a regular schedule. Most anesthesiologists work in hospitals, though they may actually be part of an individual or group practice. Others direct residents in teaching hospitals or teach at medical schools.

REQUIREMENTS

High School

If you are interested in becoming an anesthesiologist, focus your high school education on college preparatory courses. Mathematics classes and science classes, especially biology and chemistry, should be helpful. In addition, English classes will help you improve your communication and research skills. Also, consider taking a foreign language, since you may be required to show proficiency in another language later on in your schooling.

Postsecondary Training

You must first earn an M.D. or D.O. degree and pass an examination to become licensed to practice medicine. (See "Physicians" and "Osteopathic Physicians.") Then you must complete a four-year residency. The first year is spent training in an area of clinical medicine other than anesthesia, such as internal or emergency medicine, pediatrics, surgery, obstetrics, or neurology. The final three years of study are then spent in an anesthesiology residency program accredited by the Accreditation Council for Graduate Medical Education. You can find a list of accredited residency programs at the council's Web site, http://www.acgme.org.

Certification or Licensing

Anesthesiologists receive certification from the American Board of Anesthesiology. In addition to being licensed, the board requires applicants to have completed training in an accredited program and to pass an exam. Applicants must also have a certificate of clinical competence. This certificate, filed by the residency training program, attests to the applicant's clinical competence.

All physicians in the United States must be licensed to practice. Some states have reciprocity agreements with other states so that a physician licensed in one state may be automatically licensed in another without being required to pass another examination.

Other Requirements

Every surgery requires anesthesiologists to pay careful attention and to remain alert. An anesthesiologist sometimes encounters emergency situations, requiring quick, clear-headed responses. The work, however, can also be slower paced and require patience to comfort people preparing for surgery. Not only must anesthesiologists be able to explain the surgery clearly to patients, but they must be able to direct other members of the anesthesia team.

EARNINGS

Salaries for anesthesiologists vary according to the kind of practice (whether the anesthesiologist works individually or as part of a group practice), the amount of overhead required to maintain the business, and geographic location. First-year medical interns earned $47,458 in 2009, according to the Association of American Medical Colleges. Though working fewer hours, an anesthesiologist can make as much or more as other doctors. Mean annual salaries for anesthesiologists were $211,750 in 2009, according to the U.S. Department of Labor. Salaries for anesthesiologists in practice for three years or more ranged from $219,850 to $392,960, with a median salary of $301,802, according to Physicians Search, a physician recruitment agency.

Fringe benefits for physicians typically include health and dental insurance, paid vacations, and retirement plans. Self-employed anesthesiologists must provide their own benefits.

OUTLOOK

According to the *Occupational Outlook Handbook*, the field of anesthesiology is expected to grow much faster than the average for all careers through 2018. Attracted by the technological advancements, the regularity of the work, and the fewer hours, more people are entering the field. Most anesthesiologists find work immediately after finishing their residencies. As medical advances allow for different kinds of treatment facilities, anesthesiologists will find more work outside of a traditional hospital setting. The development of more outpatient clinics, freestanding surgical centers, and respiratory therapy clinics has opened up employment opportunities for anesthesiologists.

Managed care organizations have changed the way medicine is practiced and may continue to do so. Because anesthesiology is a hospital-based specialty, anesthesiologists must find ways to work within the guidelines of managed care, sometimes to the detriment of medical treatment. Anesthesiologists and other health care professionals will continue to challenge these organizations in order to practice medicine to the best of their abilities.

FOR MORE INFORMATION

For information on certification, contact
American Board of Anesthesiology
4208 Six Forks Road, Suite 900
Raleigh, NC 27609-5735
Tel: 866-999-7501
http://www.theaba.org

For information about a career as an anesthesiologist, contact
American Society of Anesthesiologists
520 North Northwest Highway
Park Ridge, IL 60068-2573
Tel: 847-825-5586
E-mail: mail@asahq.org
http://www.asahq.org

For comprehensive information on a career as an anesthesiologist and anesthesia, visit
Lifeline to Modern Medicine
http://www.lifelinetomodernmedicine.com

Ayurvedic Doctors and Practitioners

QUICK FACTS

School Subjects
Biology
Chemistry
Health

Personal Skills
Communication/ideas
Helping/teaching

Work Environment
Primarily indoors
Primarily one location

Minimum Education Level
High school diploma

Salary Range
$70,000 to $100,000 to
$250,000+

Certification or Licensing
Recommended (certification)
Required (licensing)

Outlook
Faster than the average

DOT
N/A

GOE
N/A

NOC
N/A

O*NET-SOC
N/A

OVERVIEW

Ayurvedic doctors and practitioners use theories and techniques developed thousands of years ago in India to bring people into physical, mental, emotional, and spiritual balance, thereby maintaining health, curing diseases, and promoting happiness and fulfillment. In the West, where Ayurveda is not an officially accepted and licensed form of medicine, only licensed medical doctors who are also thoroughly trained in Ayurveda can legally practice Ayurvedic medicine. These individuals are referred to as Ayurvedic doctors.

Licensed practitioners of paramedical professions, such as nutritionists, psychologists, naturopaths, massage therapists, and acupuncturists, may be called Ayurvedic practitioners if they are also trained in Ayurveda and use Ayurvedic techniques in their professional work. Any non-M.D. who practices the full range of Ayurvedic medicine in the West, however, is seen as practicing medicine without a license, which is illegal.

HISTORY

The Vedas, which may be up to 5,000 years old, are the oldest and most important scriptures of Hinduism, which is the primary religion in India. The Sanskrit word veda means "knowledge," and the Vedas contain the knowledge and beliefs on which Hinduism is based. The Atharvaveda—the Veda that deals primarily with the practical

Glossary of Ayurvedic Terms

Ahamkara: The force that forms an individual person; an individual's "I."

Ama: Toxins created by improper digestion.

Aura: The energy field that surrounds the body.

Bhavana: A process in which a mortar and pestle are used to improve the quality of a substance such as an herb.

Dosha: Any of the three forces that allow the five elements to take form as flesh.

Laxation: The use of mild laxatives to decrease an overabundant dosha.

Prajnaparadha: A condition in which a person knowingly acts in a way that harms his or her health.

Prakriti or prakruti: A person's constitution.

Prana: Life force or energy; corresponds to the Chinese term *ch'i* and the Japanese term *ki*.

Purgation: The use of strong laxatives to decrease an overabundant dosha.

Sattva: Equilibrium, balance.

Shukra: Reproductive fluids.

Tantra: A set of practices that utilize energy for spiritual purposes.

Triphala: A compound used for purification and revitalization.

Virya: The energy contained in a substance.

Yukti: A process in which an effect is caused by making various factors unite at a particular place and time.

aspects of life—contains chants, rites, and spells that are thought to enable believers to do such things as create love and goodwill among people, defeat enemies, and ensure success in agriculture. Most experts believe that the Atharvaveda is the basis of Ayurveda.

The word *Ayurveda* means "knowledge of life." The oldest of the specifically Ayurvedic texts, the *Charaka Samhita*, was written in approximately 1000 B.C. and deals with internal medicine. This and more recent texts, such as the *Astanga Hridayam*, a compilation of Ayurvedic knowledge written in approximately A.D. 1000, provide Ayurvedic practitioners with the knowledge they need to help their patients.

Ayurvedic medicine is officially accepted in India, where approximately 80 percent of those who seek medical help go to Ayurvedic doctors. In its country of origin, Ayurveda has been substantially modernized, and it now includes many techniques and medications that originated in the West. For example, in addition to ancient herbal formulas, Indian Ayurvedic doctors often prescribe antibiotics. Most Indian doctors have discarded the use of certain older practices that are described in early texts, such as the use of leeches for bloodletting.

THE JOB

Ayurveda is a way of life rather than simply a system of healing. It is a holistic system, which means that it views physical, mental, and spiritual health as intrinsically connected. An Ayurvedic doctor or practitioner treats the whole person, not simply the symptoms that a patient displays.

Ayurvedic doctors and practitioners base their treatments and recommendations on a complex body of beliefs. One of the most important beliefs holds that everything in the universe is composed of one or more of the five elements: air, fire, earth, water, and ether (space). These elements are concepts or qualities as much as they are actual entities. For example, anything that has the qualities that Ayurveda associates with fire is a manifestation of fire. A person's violent temper demonstrates the existence of fire within that person.

For the purposes of treating people, Ayurveda distills the concept of the five elements to three combinations of two elements. These are the *doshas*, which may be thought of as qualities or energies. The first dosha, Vata, is a combination of air and ether, with air predominating. The second dosha, Pitta, is a combination of fire and water, with fire predominating. The third dosha, Kapha, is a combination of water and earth, with water predominating. Every person is dominated by one or more doshas, although every person contains some element of all three. The unique combination of doshas that appears in a person is that person's *tridosha*, and that combination determines the person's constitution, or *prakriti*.

Because Ayurvedic theory holds that a person's nature and personality are based on his or her doshic makeup, or tridosha, the first thing that an Ayurvedic doctor or practitioner does when seeing a patient is to determine what that doshic makeup is. This is done by various means, including observation of physical qualities such as build, nails, lips, hair color, eye color, and skin type; taking the pulse in various locations; examination of the "nine doors," which are eyes, ears, nostrils, mouth, genitals, and anus; and questioning the patient about past history, present problems, goals, and so forth. After analyzing all this information, the practitioner determines which dosha or combination of doshas predominates in the patient's makeup.

Vata people tend to be extremely tall or extremely short and to have long fingers and toes. They are generally thin and have dark complexions and dry skin. The air element that predominates in their makeup tends to makes light, cold, and dry in various ways. They are often extremely creative, but their minds tend to flit from idea to idea, and they may be spacey and disorganized.

Pitta people, who are dominated by the fire element, are generally of medium build, and their fingers and toes are of medium length. They tend to be fair in complexion, with blond, light brown, or red hair. All redheads are said to have a significant amount of Pitta in their tridoshas. Pittas are quick to anger, can be forceful and domineering, and are highly organized. They make good engineers, accountants, and managers.

Kapha people, who are dominated by the water element, are generally large and well built, with dark hair and oily skin. Their toes and fingers are short and thick. Kaphas may gain weight easily but have great physical stamina. They are usually calm people who avoid confrontation, but once they are angered, they hold a grudge. They like routine, tend not to be extremely creative, and are reliable.

Once the practitioner has determined the patient's tridosha and has ascertained what the patient's condition, problems, and desires are, the practitioner creates a program that will improve the patient's health and well-being. One of the most important methods that the practitioner will use is diet. If the patient's tridosha is out of balance, controlled to an extreme degree by one of the doshas, the practitioner may put together a diet that will decrease that dosha and/or increase the others, gradually and safely bringing the patient to a state of balance. Ayurvedic practitioners must therefore have a thorough knowledge of foods, traditional nutrition, and cooking.

Proper eating and good digestion are extremely important in Ayurveda, but Ayurvedic practitioners also use many other methods, among which are the techniques of panchakarma, which means "five actions." Panchakarma is a powerful set of cleansing practices that is ideally undertaken only under the guidance of an Ayurvedic doctor. The treatment varies by individual, but generally a patient must undergo one to seven days of preparation before the treatment begins. The preparation involves oil massage and steam baths, which sometimes include herbal treatments. After the body is sufficiently cleansed, the panchakarma may begin.

The first of the five practices is *vamana*, which involves removing excess Kapha from the stomach by inducing vomiting by gentle means. The second practice is *virechana*, which involves using laxatives to purge the body of excess Pitta. The third and fourth practices are both forms of *vasti*, or enema therapy, in which herbal preparations are used to remove Vata from the system. One form is relatively mild; the other is stronger. The fifth practice is *nasya*, which involves ingesting liquid or powdered substances through the nose. This practice is generally used to treat illnesses that affect the head and neck. It can take up to 30 days to complete the process of panchakarma.

There are many more aspects of Ayurvedic practice, and one of the most important things that doctors and practitioners do is advise patients regarding their lifestyle. They recommend various practices, such as cleaning the tongue daily, engaging in meditation, practicing yoga, and massaging the body with oils suitable for one's tridosha and the time of year. They may even advise patients regarding what kinds of clothes are best for them and where they will be most comfortable living.

REQUIREMENTS

High School

If Ayurvedic medicine interests you, learn as much as possible about health, medicine, science, and anatomy while in high school, just as you would to prepare for a career in Western medicine. Courses in biology and chemistry are important. It will also be important to study the Hindu tradition and become familiar with Sanskrit terms. Studying Sanskrit, the language of the Vedas and the Ayurvedic texts, is a good idea, although it is not absolutely essential. Although Sanskrit is not offered in high schools, correspondence courses are available, and students in large cities may find Sanskrit courses in universities or may find teachers in an Indian community.

Postsecondary Training

Postsecondary training depends on the path you want to take. To become a full-fledged Ayurvedic doctor in the West, you must be trained as a medical doctor as well as in Ayurveda, which means getting a bachelor's degree, going to medical school, and completing an internship.

According to Scott Gerson, M.D., a fully trained Ayurvedic doctor who runs the National Institute of Ayurvedic Medicine (NIAM), specializing in internal medicine or family practice is usually the best route for those who wish to become Ayurvedic doctors, although it is possible to combine other medical specialties with Ayurvedic practice in a beneficial way. Those who wish to combine Ayurveda with careers as nutritionists, psychologists, naturopaths, and so forth must complete the educational and training requirements for those specialties as well as study Ayurveda. It is not a good idea to go into business in a Western country simply as an expert in Ayurveda, since no licensing is available and doing so may leave you open to charges of practicing medicine without a license.

The single most important part of a doctor's or practitioner's Ayurvedic training is the completion of a rigorous course of study and practice. Naturally, a student who wishes to practice should select the most comprehensive course available. An excellent way to learn Ayurveda is to study at a good Indian institution and become a full-fledged Ayurvedic doctor in India. That kind of program typically takes five years to complete and also involves supervised practice afterward. Remember, though, that being licensed in India does not make it legal to practice as a doctor in the West. Alternatively, a student may study in the West, where various institutions offer Ayurvedic training. The NIAM offers a three-year program in Ayurvedic medicine (see contact information at the end of this article).

Certification or Licensing

Ayuverdic practitioners and doctors who plan to work as physicians in the United States must take an examination to be licensed to practice. Every state requires such an examination. It is conducted through the board of medical examiners in each state. Board certification is also available in a variety of medical specialties. Those seeking to become board certified participate in residencies that last up to seven years and must pass an examination by a member board of the American Board of Medical Specialties or the American Osteophatic Association.

Other Requirements

Ayurvedic practitioners and doctors work closely with their clients, so it is essential that they be able to gain their clients' or patients' trust, make them comfortable and relaxed, and communicate effectively enough with them to gather the information that they need in order to treat them effectively. It is unlikely that an uncommunicative person who is uncomfortable with people will be able to build a successful Ayurvedic practice. In addition, a practitioner must be comfortable making decisions and working alone.

Although some jobs are available in alternative health practices, most Ayurvedic doctors and practitioners have their own practices, and anyone who sets up shop will need to deal with the basic tasks and problems that all business owners face: advertising, accounting, taxes, legal requirements, and so forth. In addition, because

Ayurveda is rooted in Hinduism, people whose religious beliefs are in conflict with Hinduism or who are uncomfortable with organized religion may be unwilling or unable to practice Ayurveda effectively.

EXPLORING

The best way to learn about Ayurveda is to speak with those who practice it. Call practitioners and ask to interview them. Find practitioners in your area if you can, but do not hesitate to contact people in other areas. There is no substitute for learning from those who actually do the work. Although many practitioners run one-person practices, it may be possible to find work of some kind with a successful practitioner or a clinic in your area, especially if you live in a large city.

You should also do as much reading as you can on the subject. Many books on Ayurveda are available. Also look for information on Ayurveda in magazines that deal with alternative medicine or Hinduism. You may also wish to read about traditional Oriental medicine, which is similar to Ayurveda in many ways.

EMPLOYERS

For the most part, Ayurvedic practitioners work for themselves, although some teach in institutions and others work for alternative clinics.

STARTING OUT

In addition to receiving training in medicine or in another professional field of your choice, you should begin by taking the best, most comprehensive Ayurvedic course of study you can find. After that, if you have not found an organization that you can work for, you should begin to practice on your own. You may rent an office or set up shop at home. Be sure to investigate the state and local laws that affect you.

A practitioner who runs his or her own business must be well versed in basic business skills. Take courses in business or get advice from the local office of the Small Business Administration. Seek advice from people you know who run their own businesses. Your financial survival will depend on your business skills, so be sure that you are as well prepared as possible.

ADVANCEMENT

Because most Ayurvedic doctors and practitioners work for themselves, advancement in the field is directly related to the quality of treatment they provide and their business skills. Ayurvedic practitioners can advance in their field by proving to the members of their community that they are skilled, honest, professional, and effective. Before they can be financially successful, there must be a strong demand for their services.

EARNINGS

Generally, Ayurvedic doctors earn what most doctors in their fields of specialty earn. The situation is the same for practitioners, who generally earn what other people in their fields earn. It is probably safe to say that Ayurvedic practitioners on the low end may make $20,000 per year and up. Practitioners typically earn from $70,000 to $100,000 annually. Doctors with Ayurvedic training may earn $250,000 or more annually.

Self-employed Ayurvedic doctors and practitioners must provide their own benefits. Those who are employed by academic institutions and alternative clinics receive benefits such as vacation days, sick leave, health and life insurance, and a savings and pension program.

WORK ENVIRONMENT

Ayurvedic practitioners usually work in their own homes or offices. Some practitioners may have office help, while others work alone. For this reason, they must be independent enough to work effectively on their own. Because they must make their clients comfortable in order to provide effective treatment, they generally try to make their workplaces as pleasant and relaxing as possible.

OUTLOOK

Although no official government analysis of the future of Ayurveda has yet been conducted, it seems safe to say that the field is expanding more rapidly than the average for all fields. Although science still views it with skepticism, Ayurveda has become relatively popular in a short period of time, largely because of the popularity of Deepak Chopra, an Ayurvedic expert who is also an M.D. It has certainly benefited from the popular acceptance of alternative medicine and therapies in recent years, particularly because it is a holistic practice that aims to treat the whole person rather than the symptoms of disease or discomfort. Because Western medicine is too often mechanical and dehumanizing, many people are looking for alternative forms of medicine.

FOR MORE INFORMATION

The AIVS provides on-site and correspondence training in Ayurveda, as well as courses in Sanskrit and other subjects of interest to Ayurvedic practitioners. It should be noted that correspondence courses do not qualify one as a practitioner, but they do prepare one for more in-depth training.

American Institute of Vedic Studies (AIVS)
PO Box 8357
Santa Fe, NM 87504-8357
Tel: 505-983-9385
E-mail: vedicinst@aol.com
http://www.vedanet.com

The Ayurvedic Institute offers both on-site and correspondence courses in Ayurveda. Some of the organization's resources are available only to those who pay a membership fee.

The Ayurvedic Institute
PO Box 23445
Albuquerque, NM 87192-1445
Tel: 505-291-9698
http://www.ayurveda.com

Deepak Chopra's Center does not offer training for practitioners, but it does offer courses for those who are interested in using Ayurveda in their own lives.

The Chopra Center
2013 Costa del Mar Road
Carlsbad, CA 92009-6801
Tel: 888-424-6772
http://www.chopra.com

The NIAM offers on-site training, sponsors correspondence courses, and sells Ayurvedic books and supplies. It offers a three-year training program in Ayurveda.

National Institute of Ayurvedic Medicine (NIAM)
584 Milltown Road
Brewster, NY 10509-5224
Tel: 845-278-8700
E-mail: ayurveda@niam.com
http://www.niam.com

Cardiologists

OVERVIEW

Cardiologists are physicians who practice in the subspecialty of internal medicine that concentrates on the diagnosis and treatment of heart disease. In most instances, cardiologists treat patients on a consultative basis to determine if the symptoms the patients are exhibiting are signs of heart disease.

HISTORY

In 1749, cardiology became a medical specialty when Jean Baptiste Senac published a comprehensive study of the heart. The development of modern cardiology heightened in 1816 when Rene Laennec invented the stethoscope. By the middle of the 19th century, the stethoscope was refined and routinely used as a diagnostic tool for the heart. Further developments, such as Carlo Matteucci's illustrated discovery of the heart's electrical charge in 1838 and Willem Einthoven's modification of the string galvanometer used to record the electrical impulses of the heart in 1903, led to the beginning stages of electrocardiography. Einthoven later refined his device and invented the electrocardiograph, an achievement that won him the Nobel Prize in 1924. Werner Forssman, Dickinson Richards, and Andre F. Cournand also won the Nobel Prize in 1956 for their use of the catheter to study the circulatory system and the heart. This achievement was made possible because of Forssman's earlier invention of the cardiac catheterization technique.

During the latter half of the 20th century, cardiology was marked by advancements in heart surgery. The first heart transplant was

Cardiologists study a patient's electrophysiology information on computer monitors to find the area of the heart that needs attention. *(Paul Tople, AP Photo*/Akron Beacon Journal)

performed by Christiaan Barnard in 1967, while the first artificial heart was used in 1982 by a team at the University of Utah. In July 2001, a man received the first completely implanted, battery-operated artificial heart in an experimental procedure at the University of Louisville.

THE JOB

During their initial consultation, cardiologists review a patient's medical history. After taking the medical history, cardiologists then perform a physical examination. This is their first opportunity to listen to the patient's heart. Often, a cardiologist can tell if there is a cardiac problem by listening to the rhythm of the heartbeat. For example, when examining a patient for a heart murmur (an abnormal sound), cardiologists will be able to tell if it is an innocent murmur, or whether it could cause problems.

There are several tests cardiologists use to aid in patient evaluation and diagnosis. The most common test is the electrocardiogram (ECG or EKG). An ECG measures the electrical activity produced by heart contractions and outputs a graph illustrating this. Many problems can be detected through ECGs.

Cardiac catheterization is another type of test. A small tube is inserted through a blood vessel into or near the heart. This procedure is used to take pictures of the heart, which cardiologists can use for diagnosis as well as to evaluate the body's electrical system and in some cases, to remove obstructions.

Another test is the echocardiogram. During this procedure, high-pitched sounds, inaudible to the human ear, are sent into the body. Their echoes are plotted by a transducer to create a picture of the heart. A stress echocardiogram evaluates the heart to measure the supply of blood going to the muscles before and after exercise.

After a diagnosis is made, cardiologists prescribe treatment, which may include drugs such as blood pressure medications or blood thinners, or lifestyle changes such as diet and exercise. If surgery is required, cardiologists refer patients to thoracic surgeons. Even though cardiologists do not perform surgery, many surgeons request cardiologists to consult in the preoperative phase of treatment.

A patient may not necessarily have symptoms of heart disease but may have risk factors. These might include a family history of heart problems, history of smoking or obesity, or presence of diseases like diabetes. In such cases, cardiologists often provide information and advice to their patients regarding the prevention of cardiac disease.

REQUIREMENTS

High School
In high school, take college preparatory classes such as biology, chemistry, physics, anatomy and physiology, and mathematics. English and speech classes will help you develop your communication skills. Other useful classes include computer science, health, psychology, and one or more foreign languages.

Postsecondary Training
Once you receive your M.D. or D.O degree and become licensed to practice medicine (see "Physicians" and "Osteopathic Physicians"), you must undertake seven to eight more years of additional training. This includes an internship that may last from one to two years and a six-year residency program. Cardiologists spend three years in a residency program in internal medicine and another three years in a residency program in the subspecialty of cardiology.

Certification or Licensing
Cardiologists should be board certified by the American Board of Internal Medicine (ABIM) in both internal medicine and then in

the cardiology subspecialty. To be certified in internal medicine, you need to have completed medical school and at least three years of additional training as well as pass a comprehensive exam. Certification in cardiology requires at least three more years of accredited training (in cardiology), proven clinical competence, and passing another comprehensive exam. The ABIM requires certified cardiologists to pursue continuing education in order to renew their certifications. This ensures that all certified doctors maintain a high level of competency. For continuing medical education, cardiologists can attend conferences, lectures, or specialized readings.

Many cardiologists choose to become members of the American College of Cardiology. Membership is a sign of a high level of professionalism and competence. To be considered for various levels of membership, the college takes into account the physician's length of service, board certifications, and scientific accomplishments. The highest level, fellow, allows the use of the initials F.A.C.C. (Fellow of the American College of Cardiology).

Other Requirements
Cardiologists need a nurturing personality. The needs of the patient must always come before their own needs. Cardiologists must be willing to put aside their own concerns while they are responsible for the care of a patient.

EARNINGS
Earnings for cardiologists vary due to factors such as the number of years the cardiologist has been in practice, the size and type of practice (private practice, large group practice, hospital, etc.), and the geographic location. First-year interns earned $47,458 in 2009, according to the Association of American Medical Colleges. The U.S. Department of Labor reports that doctors specializing in internal medicine earned mean annual salaries of $183,990 in 2009. However, cardiologists can have significantly higher earnings. Salaries for cardiologists in their first year of practice ranged from $120,000 to $250,000, according to Physicians Search, a physician recruitment agency. Those in practice for three years or more earned $205,000 to $450,607, with median annual earnings of $317,500.

Benefits will depend on the employer, but usually include such things as health insurance and retirement plans. Self-employed cardiologists must provide their own benefits.

OUTLOOK

The influence of managed care is being felt in the field of cardiology. The usual inpatient time for someone who has suffered a heart attack has been greatly reduced. Years ago it was common for heart attack patients to remain in the hospital for a month. However, inpatient hospital time has been steadily decreasing. Today it is not uncommon for a patient to stay in the hospital only five days, and sometimes just two.

Another effect of managed care is that before its introduction, it was not unusual for a patient with chest pain to automatically have an angiogram. Angiograms are very expensive, however, and doctors do not prescribe them as quickly as before.

Another influence on cardiology is the constant research that is being performed in the field. With the influx of new information, treatment processes are continually evolving. According to the U.S. Department of Labor, the employment of physicians in general is expected to increase much faster than the average for all occupations through 2018. Due to the aging population, cardiologists should continue to see a strong outlook.

FOR MORE INFORMATION

For information on certification, contact
American Board of Internal Medicine
510 Walnut Street, Suite 1700
Philadelphia, PA 19106-3699
Tel: 800-441-2246
http://www.abim.org

For information about cardiology and fellowships, contact
American College of Cardiology
Heart House
2400 N Street, NW
Washington, DC 20037-1153
Tel: 800-253-4636
http://www.acc.org

For career information, contact
Society of Thoracic Surgeons
633 North Saint Clair Street, Suite 2320
Chicago, IL 60611-3658
Tel: 312-202-5800
E-mail: sts@sts.org
http://www.sts.org

Cosmetic Surgeons

QUICK FACTS

School Subjects
Biology
Chemistry
Mathematics

Personal Skills
Leadership/management
Technical/scientific

Work Environment
Primarily indoors
Primarily multiple locations

Minimum Education Level
Medical degree

Salary Range
$125,000 to $200,000 to
$411,500+

Certification or Licensing
Required for certain
positions (certification)
Required by all states
(licensing)

Outlook
Much faster than the
average

DOT
070

GOE
14.02.01

NOC
3111

O*NET-SOC
29-1067.00

OVERVIEW

Cosmetic surgeons (also known as *plastic surgeons* and *esthetic surgeons*) are medical doctors who specialize in surgeries to correct disfigurement and/or improve physical appearance. Though the terms *cosmetic* and *plastic surgery* are often used interchangeably, cosmetic surgery usually means procedures performed to reshape normal structures of the body to improve the patient's appearance. Plastic surgery generally refers to reconstructive surgeries performed on abnormal structures of the body caused by birth defects, developmental abnormalities, trauma, injury, infection, tumors, or disease.

HISTORY

Contrary to popular belief, cosmetic surgery is not a recent development. Although the increase in the popularity of certain cosmetic procedures is a relatively new trend, surgeons have been correcting human disfigurement since 3400 B.C., when Egyptian healers performed cosmetic operations on the face, feet, and arms. Another ancient tie can be found in the profession's own name. The *plastic* in plastic surgery does not mean "artificial." Rather, plastic surgery derives its name from the ancient Greek word *plastikos*, which meant to mold or give form. In fact, the modern-day "nose job," which Hollywood celebrities seem to favor, likely got its start in ancient India, although the procedures done at that time were for reconstructive rather than strictly cosmetic purposes. By 800 B.C., physicians in India were using skin grafts (a process that transfers healthy skin from one part of the body to another for the purpose of replacing damaged or lost skin) to perform reconstructive work for facial injuries.

Cosmetic surgery changed little during the Dark Ages but began to develop again in the 1700s, when British surgeons introduced to Europe techniques they had seen in India. Further improvement in skin grafting techniques continued, but progress was slow until the early 1900s.

Before World War I, the profession evolved slowly in North America as well. Virginian Dr. John Peter Mettauer performed the first cleft palate operation in the New World in 1827 with instruments he designed himself. With the advent of world war, physicians were challenged to find ways to treat extensive facial and head injuries never before seen, such as shattered jaws and gaping skull wounds.

It was not until the late 1930s that the American Board of Surgeons, the medical certifying organization of the time, established a specialty board to certify cosmetic surgeons—the American Board of Plastic Surgery—with its own standards and specialized training. Prior to the establishment of this board, many physicians who performed reconstructive surgeries were from other specialties related to cosmetic surgery.

New techniques developed in the 1950s included internal wiring for facial fractures and rotation flaps for skin deformities. In the 1960s, the scope of procedures performed by surgeons widened as the public became more informed. Cosmetic procedures became more popular. Silicone was initially used to treat skin imperfections and was first used as a breast implant device in 1962. The 1980s saw plastic surgeons expand their efforts to bring information to the public, and in the 1990s, the profession focused efforts on having reconstructive procedures covered under health plans.

Despite the many advances, the field is still evolving. Today, researchers are trying to unlock the secrets of the growth-factor environment of the womb, where scarless healing takes place, in order to apply the technique to wounds of children and adults.

THE JOB

Doctors, especially specialists such as cosmetic surgeons, generally work long hours. Surgeries of all types demand strict attention to detail, and cosmetic surgeries in which the emphasis is on the quality of the patient's appearance can be especially challenging. Still,

Facts About Cosmetic Procedures, 2009

- $10 billion was spent on cosmetic procedures in the United States.
- The most cosmetic procedures (3.6 million) were performed in the Pacific/Mountain region of the United States.
- Females received 91 percent of all cosmetic procedures.
- Cosmetic procedures by age group: age 20–29, 734,000 total cosmetic procedures; age 30–39, 2.3 million total cosmetic procedures; age 40–54, 5.7 million total cosmetic procedures; age 55+, 3.1 million total cosmetic procedures.

Source: American Society of Plastic Surgeons

the profession offers high earnings and personal rewards. Physicians tend to be people who thrive on challenge and are willing to devote a lot of time to their careers.

Of course, cosmetic surgeons do not spend all their working hours in surgery. Daily tasks include patient consultation and record keeping, among other duties. Also, no matter what setting a surgeon practices in, he or she is likely to have administrative duties as well. Surgeons in private practice have an office to manage with duties ranging from hiring employees to marketing the practice to overseeing upkeep of the office. Surgeons who work in a hospital's plastic surgery department have commitments to the hospital outside of performing surgeries and seeing patients. For example, cosmetic surgeons frequently are required to provide general hospital emergency room coverage and split up this task with the other surgeons.

Today's cosmetic surgeons perform a wider range of procedures than their counterparts did only a few decades ago. Previously, the profession focused on reconstructive surgeries, with a few surgeons catering to those who could afford cosmetic procedures. Today, cosmetic surgeries are no longer performed on just celebrities or the wealthy. The public has become familiar with terms such as liposuction (removal of unwanted fatty deposits), implants, and facelift because those procedures have become more accessible to the general population. According to the American Society of Plastic Surgeons (ASPS), the top five surgical cosmetic procedures in 2009 were breast augmentation, nose reshaping, liposuction, eyelid surgery, and tummy tuck. And as cosmetic surgery becomes more commonplace, an increasing number of men are having it done. Nose reshaping, hair transplants, liposuction, and eyelid surgery are some of the most popular procedures among men, according to the ASPS. Today's cosmetic surgeons perform more strictly cosmetic procedures than the average cosmetic surgeon did even a decade ago.

Some surgeons still specialize in reconstructive surgery. In fact, 5.2 million reconstructive procedures were done in 2009, which suggests that there is strong demand for surgeons in this specialty. Some of the most frequent reconstructive procedures are tumor removal (mostly related to skin cancer), laceration repair, and scar revision.

There are different settings in which a cosmetic surgeon may work. Three arrangements are common. The first is private practice, in which the surgeon is the sole physician in a practice with his or her own staff. The physician performs surgeries either in his or her own clinic or at a hospital where he or she has privileges. The second is group practice, in which a surgeon is part of a group of cosmetic surgeons or other related specialists who market their services together. Group practice surgeons may also perform surgeries in their own clinic or at a hospital. The third common arrangement is working in hospital departments, where a surgeon is a member of a hospital's plastic surgery department. A less common career path for cosmetic surgeons who have considerable surgical experience are professorships at academic institutions or teaching hospitals.

Because plastic surgery is a highly specialized field, plastic surgeons generally work in urban areas, both large and small. Most rural areas don't have enough patients to create a reasonable demand.

REQUIREMENTS

High School

If you want to pursue a career in medicine, prepare yourself by learning the self-discipline to concentrate on schoolwork in high school in order to achieve the grades necessary to gain entrance to a good undergraduate program. Performing well at the college level can help you compete for slots in medical school. Start working hard in high school by taking college preparatory classes such as mathematics (including algebra and geometry) and sciences (including biology, chemistry, and physics). Also, consider taking a foreign language. Many college programs have foreign language requirements, and a familiarity with some foreign languages may help you with your medical studies later on. Finally, don't forget to take English courses. These classes will help you develop your research and writing skills—two skills that will be essential to you in your career.

In addition, check out school clubs and civic organizations that offer volunteer opportunities for students in places like local hospitals or nursing homes. In addition to the experience you will get by volunteering, you will also have the opportunity to establish valuable relationships with people who work in the health care field. Clubs such as Kiwanis, Rotary, and Lions often count community leaders such as doctors, hospital administrators, and other health care professionals among their members. Many of these clubs have charter clubs in high schools, and student members have regular contact with these community leaders.

Postsecondary Training

After earning an M.D. degree and becoming licensed to practice medicine (see "Physicians" and "Osteopathic Physicians"), new physicians must participate in a residency training program in plastic surgery. Four years of residency training is required of all surgeons certified by the American Board of Cosmetic Surgery. However, the nature of that residency training, and to some extent, the location, may be up to the individual.

Medical school graduates must apply to residency programs by ranking their preferences for different hospitals. Independent agencies, such as the National Resident Matching Program (http://www. nrmp.org), match the student's preferences with the programs for which they are qualified. Accepted residency programs are accredited by the Accreditation Council for Graduate Medical Education (http://www.acgme.org/adspublic).

Certification or Licensing

In order to receive certification from the American Board of Plastic Surgery (ABPS), a candidate must have successfully completed an approved five-year residency program in general and plastic surgery. The plastic and reconstructive surgeon then applies to the ABPS and, once the application is approved, takes the qualifying written examination. After passing the written examination, the applicant must then pass the oral examination. In order to become certified, the plastic and reconstructive surgeon must also practice the specialty of plastic surgery for two years. The candidate can take the written examination any time during the two years of practice, but the oral examination cannot be taken before the candidate has finished the two-year practice requirement.

The American Board of Cosmetic Surgery certifies physicians in the following areas: general cosmetic surgery, facial cosmetic surgery, dermatologic cosmetic surgery, and body, breast, and extremity cosmetic surgery. Requirements vary slightly for each area, but basic requirements include certification by one of the following boards recognized by the American Board of Medical Specialties, the Bureau of Osteopathic Specialists of the American Osteopathic Association, or the Royal College of Physicians and Surgeons of Canada; a one- or two-year fellowship in an approved program; proof of hospital operating room privileges; and proof of a valid medical license. Alternatively, those seeking certification must have been in practice for at least six years, have performed at least 1,000 cosmetic surgery cases, pass an oral and written examination, and be of good character.

Additionally, the American Board of Otolaryngology offers specialty certification. See For More Information for the board's contact information.

All 50 states require physicians be licensed to practice. After graduating from medical school, you need to pass the licensing examination administered through the board of medical examiners in the state where you plan to practice.

Other Requirements

The field of medicine demands highly disciplined individuals who can perform complex tasks with a high degree of accuracy. Cosmetic surgery requires skill and artistry, as well as these talents. Hard work, self-confidence, and dedication are also vital.

Medicine also requires its successful professionals to have so-called people skills in addition to knowledge and discipline. People are the "objects of the trade" for physicians, and communication skills and the ability to empathize with a wide variety of people is essential. The ability to work as part of a team is also important. A cosmetic surgeon performs surgeries and therefore depends on a surgical team to assist in surgery. The cosmetic surgeon must be able to communicate and work well with colleagues as well as patients.

EARNINGS

It takes many years of training to become a doctor, but earnings are among the highest of any occupation. For doctors, more so than for other fields, the number of years of training directly correlates with the earnings level. Specialists, such as cosmetic surgeons, generally earn more money than general practitioners. The more specialized the field, the higher the earnings.

First-year medical interns earned $47,458 in 2009, according to the Association of American Medical Colleges.

The latest data available from the U.S. Department of Labor notes that surgeons (of all types) had a mean annual income of $219,770 in 2009. Salaries for plastic surgeons in their first year of practice ranged from $125,000 to $200,000, according to Physicians Search, a physician recruitment agency. Those in practice three years or more reported earnings ranging from $196,711 to $411,500, with a median of $306,047. Cosmetic surgeons, and physicians in general, enjoy generous health care benefits. Other benefits may include recruitment bonuses, pay for continuing education, and forgiveness of school loans. Although they work long hours throughout the year, physicians are often granted several weeks paid vacation and other leave time as relief from the demanding jobs they have. Self-employed physicians must provide their own benefits.

OUTLOOK

According to the U.S. Department of Labor, the demand for physicians and surgeons is expected to grow much faster than the average for all occupations through 2018. Because of population trends that include a rapidly aging population, physicians who meet the needs of older Americans can expect to see a steady demand for their services. Cosmetic surgeons, who treat conditions associated with aging and help older people maintain a youthful appearance, can be counted among medical specialists who will be in strong demand by the aging baby boomer population.

According to statistics compiled by the ASPS, the market for these surgeons is large: In 2009, there were approximately 5.2 million reconstructive procedures done, versus approximately 1.5 million major cosmetic surgeries and approximately 11 million "minimally invasive" cosmetic procedures.

FOR MORE INFORMATION

To learn about cosmetic procedures and recent statistics, contact
American Academy of Cosmetic Surgery
737 North Michigan Avenue, Suite 2100
Chicago, IL 60611-5641
Tel: 312-981-6760
E-mail: info@cosmeticsurgery.org
http://www.cosmeticsurgery.org

For information on certification, contact
American Board of Cosmetic Surgery
http://www.americanboardcosmeticsurgery.org

For information about certification, contact
American Board of Otolaryngology
5615 Kirby Drive, Suite 600
Houston, TX 77005-2444
Tel: 713-850-0399
http://www.aboto.org

For information on certification, contact
American Board of Plastic Surgery
Seven Penn Center, Suite 400
1635 Market Street
Philadelphia, PA 19103-2204
Tel: 215-587-9322
E-mail: info@abplsurg.org
https://www.abplsurg.org

For information on aesthetic plastic surgery, contact
American Society for Aesthetic Plastic Surgery
Tel: 888-272-7711
E-mail: findasurgeon@surgery.org
http://www.surgery.org

For information about plastic surgery, contact
American Society of Plastic Surgeons
444 East Algonquin Road
Arlington Heights, IL 60005-4654
Tel: 847-228-9900
http://www.plasticsurgery.org

Dentists

QUICK FACTS

School Subjects
Chemistry
Health

Personal Skills
Helping/teaching
Technical/scientific

Work Environment
Primarily indoors
Primarily one location

Minimum Education Level
Medical degree

Salary Range
$55,250 to $166,400 to
$212,680+

Certification or Licensing
Required by all states

Outlook
Faster than the average

DOT
072

GOE
14.03.01

NOC
3113

O*NET-SOC
29-1021.00, 29-1022.00,
29-1023.00, 29-1024.00,
29-1029.0

OVERVIEW

Dentists maintain their clients' teeth through such preventive and reparative practices as extracting, filling, cleaning, or replacing teeth. They perform corrective work, such as straightening teeth, and treat diseased tissue of the gums. They also perform surgical operations on the jaw or mouth, and make and fit false teeth. Approximately 141,900 dentists work in the United States.

HISTORY

For centuries, the practice of dentistry consisted largely of curing toothaches by extraction or the use of herbs and similar methods to alleviate pain. It was practiced not only by dentists but also by barbers and blacksmiths as well. Dental care and correction have now become a sophisticated branch of medicine, and dentists are now highly trained professionals of great importance to public health.

THE JOB

General practitioners must be proficient in many areas of dentistry. They not only must handle routine treatments, such as cleaning teeth, extracting teeth, and filling cavities, but must also be on the alert for any condition in the mouth requiring special treatment, such as crooked teeth, diseased gums, and oral cancer. General practitioners must be able to use and understand X-rays and be well acquainted with laboratory work.

Most dentists are general practitioners, but almost 15 percent practice as specialists. The American Dental Association recognizes nine dental specialties: dental public health, endodontics, oral and

Did You Know?

- Dentists have been ranked in the top 10 of the most trusted and ethical professions in the United States.
- Income for dentists ranks in the top 5 percent for all careers.
- More than 40 percent of students at dental schools are women.
- Only 12 percent of dental students are minorities, although minorities make up approximately 25 percent of the U.S. population.

Source: American Dental Association, American Medical Association, U.S. Department of Labor

maxillofacial pathology, oral and maxillofacial radiology, oral and maxillofacial surgery, orthodontics and dentofacial orthopedics, pediatric dentistry, periodontics, and prosthodontics. Specialists devote their time and skills to specific dental problems. *Public health dentists* work through public health agencies to treat and educate the public on the importance of dental health and care. *Endodontists* specialize in diseases of the tooth pulp. *Oral and maxillofacial pathologists* examine and diagnose tumors and lesions of the mouth. *Oral and maxillofacial radiologists* use radiation to produce and interpret images of the oral and maxillofacial region. *Oral and maxillofacial surgeons* perform difficult tooth extractions, remove tumors from the gums or jaw, and set jaw fractures. *Orthodontists* correct irregularities in the development of teeth and jaws by means of braces and similar devices. *Pediatric dentists* specialize in the care and treatment of children's teeth. *Periodontists* treat diseased gums and other tissues that support the teeth. *Prosthodontists* design, construct, and fit dental prosthetics. The largest number of these specialists are orthodontists, followed by oral and maxillofacial surgeons, pediatric dentists, periodontists, prosthodontists, endodontists, oral and maxillofacial pathologists, oral and maxillofacial radiologists, and public health dentists.

REQUIREMENTS

High School

If you are considering a career as a dentist, be sure to study biology, chemistry, physics, health, and mathematics in high school. English and foreign language courses are also important for meeting college entrance requirements and developing good communication skills.

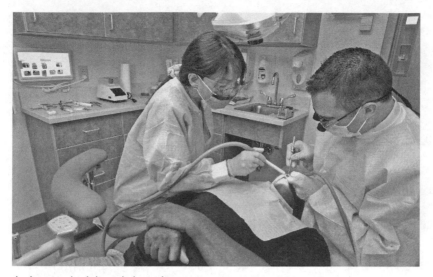

A dentist (*right*) and dental assistant treat a patient. *(D. Lassman, Syracuse Newspapers, The Image Works)*

Participation in extracurricular activities will also enhance your background because it provides opportunities to interact with many different people and develop interpersonal skills.

Postsecondary Training
The dental profession is selective, and standards are high. Your college grades and the amount of college education you have completed at the time of application are carefully considered in the admissions process for dental school. In addition, all dental schools approved by the American Dental Association (ADA) require applicants to pass the Dental Admissions Test, which gauges a student's prospects of success or failure in dental school. Information on tests and testing centers may be obtained from the Council on Dental Education and Licensure of the ADA.

Dental schools require at least two years of college-level predental education. However, about 80 percent of students entering dental schools have already earned a bachelor's or master's degree. Professional training in a dental school generally requires four academic years. Many dental schools have an interdisciplinary curriculum in which the dental student studies basic science with students of medicine, pharmacy, and other health professions. Clinical training is frequently begun in the second year. Most schools now feature a department of community dentistry, which involves a study of communities, urban problems, and sociology, and includes treatment of patients from the community. Generally the degree of doctor of dental surgery (D.D.S.) is granted upon graduation, although some schools give the degree of doctor of dental medicine (D.D.M. or D.M.D.).

Dental students who wish to enter a specialized field should plan on postgraduate study ranging from two to five years. A specialist can only become certified by passing specialty board exams. A dentist may obtain further training as a dental intern or resident in an approved hospital. Dentists must continually keep abreast of developments in the profession by reading professional magazines and journals, taking short-term graduate courses, and participating in seminars.

Certification or Licensing

All 50 states and the District of Columbia require dentists to be licensed. To qualify for a license in most states, a candidate must graduate from a dental school accredited by the American Dental Association's Commission on Dental Accreditation and pass written and practical examinations. Candidates may fulfill the written part of the exam by passing the National Board Dental Examinations. Individual states or regional testing agencies give the written or practical examinations. Generally, dentists licensed in one state are required to take another exam to practice in another state. Approximately 20 states grant licenses to dentists from other states based on their credentials. Dentists who intend to practice in a specialty area must be licensed or certified in all 50 states.

Other Requirements

Manual dexterity and scientific ability are important. Skilled, steady hands are necessary, as are good spatial judgment and some artistic ability. Good vision is required because of the detailed work. Strong communication skills are necessary to interact well with patients and coworkers.

EXPLORING

You might be able to gain an awareness of the demands of dentistry by observing a dentist at work. Work as a dental hygienist, dental assistant, or dental laboratory technician might lead to continued study in dentistry. Because of the nature of dentistry, developing good manual dexterity through sculpting or metalworking would be helpful to the prospective dentist. Also, consider volunteering in any medical environment to gain a feel for medical work. Even if you volunteer at a local hospital, for example, you'll be able to work around medical staff and discover firsthand how it feels to help people. Reading books and visiting Web sites about dentistry are other good ways to learn more about the field.

EMPLOYERS

Nearly all of the 141,900 dentists in the United States are in private practice. Of the remainder, about half work in research or teaching, or hold administrative positions in dental schools. Other opportunities for dentists can be found in the armed forces, public health services, hospitals, and clinics. Slightly more than 80 percent of all dentists are general practitioners; the rest are specialists.

The expense of pursuing an education in dentistry and setting up a practice is significant. However, in a survey reported in the magazine *Inc.*, dental offices were the third-highest ranking category of start-up businesses most likely to survive. According to the ADA, among dentists out of dental school less than four years, about 42 percent owned their practice; by six years after graduation, 53 percent had their own practices.

STARTING OUT

Once a dentist has graduated from an approved dental school and passed a state licensing examination, there are three common avenues of entry into private practice. A dentist may open a new office, purchase an established practice, or join another dentist or group of dentists to gain further experience. There are, however, other choices for licensed dentists. They may enter the armed forces as commissioned officers, or, through civil service procedures, become eligible for work in the U.S. Public Health Service. They may also choose to work in hospitals, clinics, or schools. For some, work in a dental laboratory or teaching dentistry will provide a satisfying career.

ADVANCEMENT

Advancement for the newly licensed dentist in private practice depends on his or her personal skill in handling patients as well as dental work. Through the years, the successful dentist builds a reputation and thus advances with a growing clientele. The quality of the work depends in part on an ability to keep up with developments in the field. For salaried dentists in the various areas of employment, advancement will also depend on the quality and skill of their work. Advancement may take the form of a step from general practitioner to specialist, a step requiring further study and generally providing higher income. Teachers may look forward to administrative positions or to appointments as professors.

Success may also depend on the location of the practice; people in higher-income areas are more likely to request dental care. In small towns and sparsely populated areas, a great need exists for dentists, and competition is slight. In cities where there are many dentists, it may be more difficult to establish a practice despite the larger pool of possible patients.

EARNINGS

Beginning dentists, faced with the expense of buying equipment and the problem of establishing a practice, generally earn enough to cover expenses and little more. However, income rises rapidly as the dentist's practice becomes established. According to the U.S. Department of Labor, the average annual earnings of dentists in general practice were about $142,090 a year in 2009, while specialists averaged more than $212,680 per year. According to the U.S. Department of Labor, orthodontists had mean annual incomes of $206,190 in 2009. Some dentists earned less than $55,250. Dentists' earnings are lower during economic downturns, when people tend to postpone dental treatment except for emergencies.

Benefits for salaried dentists include vacation and sick time, health insurance, and sometimes and pension or 401(k) plans. Dentists who operate their own practices must provide their own benefits.

WORK ENVIRONMENT

Because most dentists are in private practice, they are free to set their hours and establish offices according to their individual tastes. Most dentists work from four to five days a week, many times averaging 40 or more hours. They spend about 90 percent of their time treating patients. The beginning dentist must set aside expensive decorating plans in favor of suitable equipment, but most dentists' offices are designed to be pleasant and comfortable. Dentists may employ dental assistants, hygienists, or laboratory technicians, or they may carry out the special duties of each themselves. However, there is a growing trend to leave simpler tasks, such as teeth cleaning and other duties, to dental hygienists and assistants, so dentists have more time to perform higher paying procedures, such as root canals.

The dentist in private practice sets individual hours and practices after office hours only in emergencies. Salaried dentists working for a clinic, hospital, or the Public Health Service are subject to conditions set by their employers.

OUTLOOK

Employment of dentists is expected to grow faster than the average for all occupations through 2018, according to the U.S. Department of Labor. Many positions will open as a result of the need to replace the large number of dentists who reach retirement age or who choose to stay in practice while reducing their office hours.

Additionally, opportunities for specialists, such as cosmetic dentists, will be very good. Three-fourths of American adults believe that a winning smile is related to job success. Most adults are unhappy with their teeth, creating a demand for dentists skilled in cosmetic techniques such as bleaching and veneering. People are concerned about dental health and can usually afford dental care, especially as dental insurance becomes more readily available. Cosmetic dentists will be in demand especially in large metropolitan areas such as Los Angeles and Chicago.

Scientific advances in the field offer a promising future for specialists. The work of the oral pathologist or orthodontist, for example, will increase as people become more aware of the need for such care. Public health programs, too, can be expected to expand. Dentistry today is focusing more on preventive care than reparative practice.

Admission to dental school is extremely is competitive. High school students must be aware of the importance of maintaining high grades if they wish to qualify. The number of new graduates entering the field each year is larger than the number of openings. Dentists rarely leave the profession except to retire, and many continue to work beyond retirement age, simply reducing the number of hours they work.

FOR MORE INFORMATION

The ADA has information on dental careers, education requirements, and dental student membership.
    American Dental Association (ADA)
    211 East Chicago Avenue
    Chicago, IL 60611-2678
    Tel: 312-440-2500
    http://www.ada.org

For information on admission requirements of U.S. and Canadian dental schools, contact
    American Dental Education Association
    1400 K Street, NW, Suite 1100
    Washington, DC 20005-2415
    Tel: 202-289-7201
    http://www.adea.org

Dermatologists

OVERVIEW

Dermatologists study, diagnose, and treat diseases and ailments of the skin, hair, mucous membranes, nails, and related tissues or structures. They may also perform cosmetic services, such as scar removal or hair transplants.

HISTORY

Many in the medical profession opposed specialization when it began to occur in the 19th century. They thought treatments would be too fragmented for patients' own good. There were several factors, however, that made specialization inevitable. The amount of medical information was increasing and complex new techniques were developing at such a rapid pace that doctors could not keep up with the advances. They began to send patients to physicians who concentrated on one type of illness or manipulation. Specialization was also attractive because it gave doctors the opportunity to demand higher fees, work fewer hours, and command greater respect from peers and the public. Medical experts gradually abandoned their ideas that general disease was caused by problems of the humors, or elemental fluids of the body, and began to diagnose and treat local organs instead.

The specialty of dermatology had its beginnings in the mid-1800s in Vienna when a doctor named Ferdinand von Hebra, one of the first to specialize entirely in skin diseases, founded a division of dermatology. At that time, medicine concentrated primarily on abnormalities in the four humors—blood, phlegm, black bile, and yellow bile—and they believed symptoms were caused by

QUICK FACTS

School Subjects
Biology
Chemistry

Personal Skills
Helping/teaching
Technical/scientific

Work Environment
Primarily indoors
Primarily multiple locations

Minimum Education Level
Medical degree

Salary Range
$120,000 to $225,000 to $407,000+

Certification or Licensing
Required for certain positions (certification)
Required by all states (licensing)

Outlook
Much faster than the average

DOT
070

GOE
14.02.01

NOC
3111

O*NET-SOC
29-1067.00, 29-1069.02

those abnormalities. Hebra made classifications based on changes in the tissues instead of on symptoms or on general disease categories. As a result, his treatment was directed toward the local problem rather than treating imbalances in the humors. He was responsible for the discovery that scabies was transmissible from person to person and could be cured by the destruction of the itch-mite parasite.

Innumerable discoveries have been made in the field of dermatology, including new medicines, treatments, and equipment. Lasers and computer technology, for example, have drastically changed dermatology, improving diagnostic techniques and allowing certain surgical procedures to be performed without using a scalpel.

THE JOB

Dermatologists study, diagnose, and treat diseases and ailments of the largest, most visible organ of the body, the skin, and its related tissues and structures: hair, mucous membranes, and nails. Their work begins with diagnosis to determine the cause of the disease or condition. This process involves studying a patient's history, conducting visual examinations, and taking blood samples, smears of the affected skin, microscopic scrapings, or biopsy specimens of the skin. They may order cultures of fungi or bacteria, or perform patch and photosensitivity tests to reveal allergies and immunologic diseases. They may also evaluate bone marrow, lymph nodes, and endocrine glands. Usually dermatologists send skin, tissue, or blood specimens to a laboratory for chemical and biological testing and analysis.

Dermatologists treat some skin problems with prescribed oral medications, such as antibiotics, or topical applications. Certain types of eczema and dermatitis, psoriasis, acne, or impetigo can usually be treated with creams, ointments, or oral medicines.

Exposure to ultraviolet light is used to treat such conditions as psoriasis, and radiation therapy is occasionally used to treat keloids (scar tissue that grows excessively).

Some skin conditions and illnesses require surgical treatment. There are three types of skin cancer—basal cell carcinoma, squamous cell carcinoma, and malignant melanoma—which must be removed surgically. Dermatologists may use traditional surgery, where the cancerous cells and surrounding tissue are cut away, but some cancers can be removed by lasers, frozen by cryosurgery, destroyed with a cautery device (high-frequency electric current), or destroyed by radiation therapy. Another type of surgery dermatologists use is Moh's surgery, in which progressive layers of skin and tissue are cut out and examined microscopically for the presence of cancers. Dermatologists also perform skin graft procedures to repair wounds that are too large to be stitched together. After removal of a skin tumor, for example, they take a portion of skin from another part of the patient's body, such as the thigh, and attach it to the wound. Since the skin graft comes from the patient's own body, there is no problem with rejection.

Not all surgeries that dermatologists perform are major. There are many conditions that can be treated with simple outpatient procedures under local anesthetic, including removal of warts, sebaceous cysts, scars, moles, cosmetic defects of the skin, boils, and abscesses. Hair transplants are usually done in the doctor's office, as are laser treatments for disfiguring birth defects, cysts, birthmarks, spider veins, and growths.

Certain diseases can manifest themselves in a skin condition. When dermatologists see that a skin problem is a sign of an illness in another part of the patient's body, they recommend treatment by other specialists. If a patient complains of itchy or scaly skin, for example, it may be an allergy. Boils may be a sign of diabetes mellitus, and a skin rash may indicate secondary syphilis. Dermatologists must often consult with allergists, internists, and other doctors. In turn, many dermatologists are called on by other specialists to help diagnose complicated symptoms.

Dermatologists not only deal with the physical aspects of skin afflictions, but the emotional aspects, too. Patients often have to face embarrassment, ridicule, and rejection because of their skin ailments, and dermatologists can help them overcome this kind of trauma.

Within the field of dermatology there are some subspecialties. *Dermatoimmunologists* focus on the treatment of diseases that involve the immune system, including allergies. They may use a procedure called immunofluorescence to diagnose and characterize these skin disorders. *Dermatopathologists* study the tissue structure and features of skin diseases. *Dermatologic surgeons* perform Moh's micrographic surgery and cosmetic procedures, including collagen injections, sclerotherapy (the injection of varicose veins with a fluid), and dermabrasion (a planing of the skin using sandpaper, wire brushes, or other abrasive materials). *Pediatric dermatologists* treat skin disorders in children. *Occupational dermatologists* study and treat occupational disorders, such as forms of dermatitis from chemical or biological irritants.

Some dermatologists combine a private practice with a teaching position at a medical school. Others are involved in research, developing new treatments, and finding cures for skin ailments. A few work in industry, developing cosmetics, lotions, and other consumer products.

REQUIREMENTS

High School

Dermatologists, like all physicians, have completed a great deal of education. You should realize that after high school your education will continue on through college, medical school, and a residency in your specialty. In high school you can start preparing for both college and your medical studies by taking science classes such as biology, chemistry, physics, and anatomy. Mathematics classes, such as algebra and geometry, will give you experience in working with numbers and formulas, both important skills for this career. Make sure your high school education is well rounded and college preparatory by taking English and history classes as well as a foreign language. Also, psychology classes and other social science classes may give you a background in understanding people—an important skill for any doctor. Take this time to develop your study habits and determine how well you like the course of study.

Postsecondary Training

After earning an M.D. or D.O. degree and becoming licensed to practice medicine (see "Physicians" and "Osteopathic Physicians"), dermatologists must complete a residency that lasts a minimum of four years, three of which are spent specializing in dermatology. The first year is a clinical residency program in internal medicine, family practice, general surgery, or pediatrics. The next three years are spent studying and practicing dermatology. Residents are closely supervised as they study skin pathology, bacteriology, radiology, surgery, biochemistry, allergy and immunology, and other basics. Intensive laboratory work in mycology (the study of the fungi that infect humans) is usually required. Following the residency, dermatologists can become certified by the American Board of Dermatology and have full professional standing.

Certification or Licensing

Certification in dermatology, as mentioned above, is given by the American Board of Dermatology. Although certification is voluntary, it is strongly recommended. Certification demonstrates the physician's dedication to the field, assures patients of his or her educational qualifications, and affirms that the physician has met the American Board of Dermatology's standards to practice this specialty. To qualify for certification, you must have completed your residency and pass written and sometimes practical examinations given by the American Board of Dermatology. Subspecialty certifications are also available from the board.

All physicians in the United States must be licensed to practice. Some states have reciprocity agreements with other states so that a physician licensed in one state may be automatically licensed in another without being required to pass another examination.

Other Requirements

Medical school and the dermatological residency are filled with stress and pressure, and they are also physically demanding. Residents often work 30-hour shifts and put in as many as 80 hours a week. They need to be emotionally stable in order to handle the stress of this intense schedule. Physicians need self-confidence because they make decisions on critical medical issues. They must also have keen observation skills, be detail oriented, and have excellent memories. Finally, because this is a "people job," physicians need to be able to relate to people with compassion and understanding.

EARNINGS

Earnings for dermatologists are affected by number of years in practice, geographic region, hours worked, and the skill, personality, and professional standing of the doctor. First-year interns earned $47,458 in 2009, according to the Association of American Medical Colleges. Salaries for dermatologists in their first year of practice ranged from $120,000 to $225,000, with median annual earnings of $160,000, according to Physicians Search, a physician recruitment agency. Those in practice three years or longer reported earnings ranging from $168,988 to $407,000, with median annual earnings of $232,000.

Dermatologists in private practice or group partnerships have the potential for higher earnings, but they must cover all of their own business expenses and benefits. For those hired by health care organizations, in addition to salary, dermatologists may receive benefits, including health and life insurance, malpractice liability insurance, paid vacation, and retirement plans. Some earn productivity bonuses as well.

OUTLOOK

The health care industry is thriving, and the U.S. Department of Labor predicts that employment for physicians will grow much faster than the average for all occupations through 2018. The field of dermatology is expected to expand for a number of reasons. New technologies, medicines, and treatments continue to be developed at a rapid pace.

Another factor in the growth of this industry is that the average age of the American population is rising, and older people require more skin-related health care. Demand for dermatologists has increased as people have become aware of the effects of radiation exposure from the sun and of air pollutants on skin. The public is also much more aware of the benefits of good general and dermatological health.

FOR MORE INFORMATION

The AAD can provide good medical information on dermatological conditions as well as employment opportunities and professional concerns.

American Academy of Dermatology (AAD)
PO Box 4014
Schaumburg, IL 60618-4014
Tel: 866-503-7546
http://www.aad.org

For information on certification and careers, contact
American Board of Dermatology
Henry Ford Health System
1 Ford Place
Detroit, MI 48202-3450
Tel: 313-874-1088
E-mail: abderm@hfhs.org
http://www.abderm.org

━━━━━━ INTERVIEW ━━━━━━

Dr. Sandra Marchese Johnson is a dermatologist in Fort Smith, Arkansas. She discussed her career with the editors of Careers in Focus: Physicians.

Q. Please tell us a little about yourself. What made you want to become a dermatologist?

A. I knew at the age of five years old that I wanted to be a doctor. My exposure to physicians was only to my pediatrician since there are no medical personnel in my family. So I thought all physicians were pediatricians. It was, however, during my second year of medical school while we were studying the skin that I became so excited to learn about the skin, and I realized my passion in life. From that point on, I knew I wanted to be a dermatologist. I then shadowed a local dermatologist, Dr. Bob

Brodell, who has been my lifelong mentor. One of my best professional accomplishments is that I wrote a textbook (*Warts: Diagnosis and Management: An Evidence-Based Approach*) about warts with Dr. Brodell. I have been practicing dermatology since 1996 and am still passionate about skin.

My husband is also a dermatologist, and we practice together. You can view our Web site by visiting http://www.johnson dermatology.com.

Q. What is one thing that young people may not know about a career in dermatology?

A. You can specialize in dermatology into dermatologic surgery (my husband did an extra two years of training in skin surgery), lasers, cosmetic dermatology, pediatric dermatology, geriatric dermatology, dermatopathology, etc. My practice is about 40 percent cosmetic dermatology, 30 percent medical dermatology, 20 percent pediatric dermatology, and 10 percent dermatologic research with clinical trials.

Q. What skills and experiences will prepare students for residency training?

A. After graduating from medical school, there is usually a four-year postgraduate residency training program in dermatology. Dermatology residencies are very competitive, so having the highest grades and test scores possible as well as participating in research and extracurricular activities are important to help you stand out from the crowd of other applicants.

Q. What are some of the pros and cons of your job?

A. I love my job. I do not think of it, however, as a job. I think of it as being fortunate to make a good living getting to do what I love. I am very passionate about what I do. I love what I do. You can see the results of what we do in dermatology. With a few simple cosmetic procedures we can make pretty people even prettier. We can improve acne, rid warts, and remove skin cancer. The results are visible and rewarding. We often develop long-term relationships with our patients. Dermatology is happy medicine.

Q. What is the future employment outlook for dermatologists?

A. There is a shortage of dermatologists nationally. I think this will continue since there are only a handful of new dermatology residents graduating every year. The future is bright!

Ear, Nose, and Throat Specialists

QUICK FACTS

School Subjects
  Biology
  Health

Personal Skills
  Helping/teaching
  Technical/scientific

Work Environment
  Primarily indoors
  Primarily multiple
    locations

Minimum Education Level
  Medical degree

Salary Range
  $120,000 to $195,000 to
  $392,890+

Certification or Licensing
  Required for certain
    positions (certification)
  Required by all states
    (licensing)

Outlook
  Much faster than the
    average

DOT
  070

GOE
  14.02.01

NOC
  3112

O*NET-SOC
  29-1067.00, 29-1069.00

OVERVIEW

An ear, nose, and throat (ENT) specialist, or otolaryngologist, provides comprehensive medical and surgical care for patients with diseases and disorders that involve or affect the ears, nose, throat, and related structures of the head and neck. Fifty percent of all physician office visits are for ear, nose, and throat illnesses. Many ENT specialists operate in private practices, and some work in large academic/university settings where they help train medical students and residents.

HISTORY

Ear, nose, and throat, or otolaryngology, is the oldest medical specialty in the United States. Otolaryngologists manage diseases of the ears, nose, nasal passages, sinuses, larynx (voice box), and oral cavity and upper pharynx (mouth and throat) as well as structures of the neck and face.

THE JOB

Ear, nose, and throat specialists deal with problems as varied as adenoid infections, allergies, earaches, earwax buildup, hay fever, snoring, and many far more serious conditions or diseases such as throat, ear, mouth, thyroid, voice box, face, and neck cancer. They practice in the following subspecialties: pediatric otolaryngology (children), otology/neurotology (balance, ears,

Did You Know?

- Fifty percent of all physician office visits are for ear, nose, and throat illnesses.
- Hearing loss affects 10 percent of North Americans.
- Approximately 35 million people in the United States develop chronic sinusitis annually.

Source: American Academy of Otolaryngology–Head and Neck Surgery

and tinnitus), facial plastic and reconstructive surgery, head and neck, allergy, laryngology (throat), and rhinology (nose). The ENT specialist usually sees patients in a clinic or office setting to evaluate symptoms that affect their ears, nose, throat, and related structures of the head and neck.

Otolaryngologists work closely with other physicians, sometimes referring patients to other specialists. Frequently they work with other medical specialties to solve single or multiple medical issues or to perform extensive surgery. For instance, some ENT specialists may be trained to perform reconstructive surgery using skin flaps or grafts to close a hole created by the removal of a tumor. Other surgical procedures, such as a cochlear implant, may help a patient regain some hearing and be able to communicate better.

In addition to working as practicing physicians, ENT specialists also teach otolaryngology at colleges and universities.

REQUIREMENTS

High School
Recommended high school classes include anatomy and physiology, biology, chemistry, physics, mathematics, English, speech classes, computer science, health, psychology, and one or more foreign languages.

Postsecondary Training
After receiving a medical degree and becoming licensed to practice medicine (see "Physicians" and "Osteopathic Physicians"), medical students who have decided to go into otolaryngology are required to complete five years of residency (one year of study in general surgery

as their internship and a four-year residency program in otolaryngology—head and neck surgery). At the end of the five-year postgraduate training, an ENT specialist who wants to subspecialize completes additional training through fellowships in specialties such as facial plastic surgery, voice ENT, voice disorders, rhinology, otology, and head and neck cancer.

Certification or Licensing

The American Board of Otolaryngology certifies physicians in otolaryngology and its subspecialty fields. In order to be a candidate for certification in otolaryngology, a physician must have successfully completed medical school and five years of residency training in otolaryngology—head and neck surgery. The certification requires passing a two-part examination.

All physicians in the United States must be licensed to practice. Some states have reciprocity agreements with other states so that a physician licensed in one state may be automatically licensed in another without being required to pass another examination.

Other Requirements

To be a successful ENT specialist, you should be a good clinician, pay close attention to detail, and have good hand-eye coordination and manual dexterity. Other important attributes include being a good listener and having good communication skills. You should also enjoy working with people and respect your patients. Being imaginative and adaptable is also a good trait for this profession.

EARNINGS

Earnings vary according to geographical region, type and size of practice, hours worked per week, and professional reputation. First-year medical interns earned $47,458 in 2009, according to the Association of American Medical Colleges. According to Physicians Search, a physician recruitment agency, ENT specialists in their first year of practice earned salaries that ranged from $120,000 to $195,000, with median annual earnings of $175,000. Those in practice three years or more reported earnings of $180,084 to $392,890, with a median of $264,878.

Benefits for ear, nose, and throat specialists include vacation and sick time, health, and sometimes dental, insurance, and pension or 401(k) plans. Those who have their own practices must provide their own benefits.

OUTLOOK

Overall, the health care industry is thriving, and the employment of physicians in almost all fields is expected to grow much faster than the average through 2018. The expertise of the ENT specialist will always be in great demand. The specialty is gaining more and more attention, especially as more ENT specialists are appointed as the heads of medical schools and residency programs.

FOR MORE INFORMATION

For information about otolaryngology careers and training, contact
American Academy of Otolaryngology–Head and Neck Surgery
1650 Diagonal Road
Alexandria, VA 22314-2857
Tel: 703-836-4444
http://www.entnet.org

For information about certification, contact
American Board of Otolaryngology
5615 Kirby Drive, Suite 600
Houston, TX 77005-2444
Tel: 713-850-0399
http://www.aboto.org

For information about membership for surgeons, contact
American College of Surgeons
633 North Saint Clair Street
Chicago, IL 60611-3211
Tel: 312-202-5000
E-mail: postmaster@facs.org
http://www.facs.org

For information on head and neck cancer, contact
American Head and Neck Society
11300 West Olympic Boulevard, Suite 600
Los Angeles, CA 90064-1663
Tel: 310-437-0559
E-mail: admin@ahns.info
http://www.headandneckcancer.org

Emergency Room Physicians

OVERVIEW

Emergency room physicians provide immediate care to critically ill or injured persons, usually in hospital emergency rooms. There are approximately 27,000 emergency room physicians in the United States.

HISTORY

As important as emergency medicine is, it is relatively new as a distinct medical specialty. The American College of Emergency Physicians was founded in 1968. The first specialist residency program was established in 1970, and the American Board of Medical Specialists authorized the first certification tests in 1979. Emergency rooms need specially qualified doctors because external injuries may hide a life-threatening injury. Internal injuries to vital organs may be overlooked by a doctor not trained to spot them. Medical professionals call the first hour after an accident the "Golden Hour." If a patient can make it to treatment within that hour, his or her chances of surviving even the most serious medical problems increase dramatically. A web of highly skilled professionals, including emergency medical technicians and emergency room nurses, works to ensure the quickest possible transport and treatment of these cases. At the center of it all is the emergency room physician.

THE JOB

Emergency room physicians (ERPs) are specialists who treat victims of accidents or sudden illnesses. They are responsible for these persons from the time they come into the emergency room (or other facility) until they are medically stable and can be either admitted to the hospital or sent home.

In low-income neighborhoods, where people are less likely to have medical insurance or a family doctor, emergency rooms often function as nonemergency clinics. ERPs may see a baby with a bad cold, stitch up a cut lip, admit a person with chest pains, and treat a gunshot wound, all in the same day. Not all emergency rooms have the same capabilities. In every case, though, the ERP's job is the same—stabilize patients until they can be moved safely.

ERPs do not just see dramatic cases. They also handle emergencies that are not life threatening. There are many minor accidents requiring treatment that can be taken care of in the ER without having to admit the patient into the hospital. Sprained ankles are wrapped or splinted, cuts are stitched, and prescriptions are given for minor illnesses or for pain. No matter what the patient's complaint, the ERP must make quick, accurate judgments about the nature of the problem and the correct treatment. This process includes taking the patient's medical history, ordering tests, and giving medication. In addition to these duties, ERPs keep a running account of everything that occurs in the ER: tests ordered, test results, drugs administered, and any changes in the patient's condition.

ERPs do not work alone, of course. They operate as the head of a team. While on duty, the ERP is responsible for everything that goes on in the ER. ERPs must be able to work well with others and inspire the confidence of the people working with them.

Emergency room doctors must be able to work quickly and accurately under stress. The pressure can be intense. At times, several patients will be waiting for treatment at once and the doctor may have to move back and forth between them. Doctors must be ready to make decisions that can mean the difference between life and death. Communications with staff, patients, and family are critical. Instructions to staff must be clear. Patients are often the only source of such vital information as their medical history and the circumstances of their injury. The ERP must be able to gain their trust quickly so that no time is wasted. It is also the doctor's job to speak to the patients' loved ones, letting them know what is happening and why. In order to keep everything running smoothly, ERPs must balance all these responsibilities.

Treating a variety of cases is just one of the many ways emergency room doctors' activities differ from those of other physicians. For one thing, ERPs work set shifts of eight, 10, or 12 hours, depending on the hospital. The ER is staffed 24 hours a day, seven days a week, so some weekend and night shifts are required. In comparison, doctors with regular practices work very long hours, and surgeons and other specialists may be called in to the hospital at any time.

A typical ERP works four or five shifts a week, depending on the length of the shift. The work is physically demanding. The stress of making life and death decisions takes a physical and psychological toll. While the ERP's work schedule (the number of shifts a person works in a given week) is very predictable, the workload (the number of cases seen during a given shift) is not.

The stress is great at times, and the volume of patients is high, but ER doctors tend to remain in emergency medicine for a long time.

REQUIREMENTS

High School
You can begin preparing for medical school studies while you are still in high school. Get a solid background in the sciences by taking core courses, including biology, chemistry, and physics. Take mathematics classes such as algebra, geometry, and trigonometry, as well as history and computer science courses. English classes will help you develop those important communication skills. Unlike some professions, where high school merely gives a basis for later learning, medical students will use their science training continuously throughout their schooling and into their professional lives. This is not to say that academics are the only area you should concentrate on. You should strive to be well rounded at all levels. Physicians have to really want to help people. The best students do not always make the best doctors, not if they cannot relate to their patients. Volunteering in a local hospital is a good way to see if medicine is the career for you, and it helps develop aspects of your personality that academic studies don't.

Postsecondary Training
Beginning with medical school, competition for available positions is tremendous. Many more applications are received by medical schools than there are positions available. Achieving excellent grades in college is your first step on the road to acceptance at the medical school of your choice.

It is not necessary for students to follow a premedical course of study in college. Many future doctors majored in liberal arts or other fields before going on to medical school. Nevertheless, you will need to take all the required sciences, including organic and inorganic chemistry, biology, microbiology, and anatomy. Again, it is important for students to maintain good grades. According to the Emergency Medicine Residents' Association (EMRA), some students interested in emergency medicine get a taste of the field by becoming emergency medical technicians while still in college. One requirement for entering medical school is to take the Medical College Admission Test (MCAT). Students often take the MCAT in their third year of undergraduate study. MCAT test scores, college transcripts, and letters of recommendation are sent in with their applications to medical schools. At least one interview with a member of the college is usually required. In addition to academics, medical schools consider factors such as personality, character, and extracurricular activities, such as volunteer work in health care settings.

After earning a M.D. or D.O. degree and becoming licensed to practice medicine (see "Physicians" and "Osteopathic Physicians"), ERPs participate in a three-year residency in emergency medicine. The EMRA offers information on residency programs at its Web site, http://www.emra.org.

Certification or Licensing

Certification, which is given by the American Board of Emergency Medicine (ABEM), is not currently required for this work, but it is highly recommended. With ABEM certification you will enhance your chances of getting the best jobs and advancing in the profession. To obtain certification, ABEM requires emergency room doctors to have completed a three-year residency and pass both written and oral exams. Subspecialty certification is available in medical toxicology, pediatric emergency medicine, sports medicine, undersea and hyperbaric medicine, and hospice and palliative medicine.

All states require physicians to be licensed before they can practice. In order to be licensed, doctors must have graduated from medical school, passed the licensing test, and completed their residency.

Other Requirements

Perhaps the most critical trait for those wanting to become physicians is a powerful drive to succeed. Demanding professions require exceptional individuals, and few professions are as demanding as emergency room medicine. Doctors first and foremost must be excellent students. They must master vast amounts of information, and the learning does not stop with graduation. They have to learn new information constantly. Hard work and a keen mind are only the beginning. As noted before, ERPs are subjected to enormous stress. How they deal with stress will determine how successful they are in the emergency room. They must project a calm, confident manner in a crisis, because the staff, the patient, and the patient's family are looking to the doctor for answers and support. They must remain calm in the midst of emotional turmoil, and be ready to make decisions without consulting with other physicians. ERPs must have fairly strong egos. They must believe in themselves and in their abilities. Emergency medical situations push doctors to the limit, and persons wishing to work in this atmosphere must be prepared to give their maximum effort.

Communication skills are an important part of any physician's practice, but the special requirements of emergency medicine make them vital to the ERP. Whether giving instructions to staff, getting vital information from a patient, or consulting with family members, the ERP is always communicating. Half of communication is listening, so ERPs must be able to concentrate in the midst of confusion.

EARNINGS

All physicians are well paid. Specialists, like emergency room doctors, are even more highly valued. Salaries for ERPs in their first year of practice ranged from $145,000 to $200,000, according to Physicians Search, a physician recruitment agency. Those in practice three years or longer reported annual earnings of $160,00 to $250,000, with median earnings of $210,830. First-year medical interns earned $47,458 in 2009, according to the Association of American Medical Colleges.

Benefits for ERPs depend on the employer; however, they usually include such items as health insurance, retirement or 401(k) plans, and paid vacation days.

OUTLOOK

Employment for physicians is expected to grow much faster than average for all careers through 2018, according to the U.S. Department of Labor. Strong employment growth is expected for emergency room physicians. The American College of Emergency Physicians says that the number of new graduates in emergency medicine is lower than the number of emergency room doctors needed to staff emergency facilities. Opportunities should be best in rural areas and the central portion of the United States.

FOR MORE INFORMATION

For information about certification, contact
American Board of Emergency Medicine
3000 Coolidge Road
East Lansing, MI 48823-6319
Tel: 517-332-4800
E-mail: abem@abem.org
http://www.abem.org

Visit the college's Web site for information about membership and to read Building Your Career in Emergency Medicine.
American College of Emergency Physicians
PO Box 619911
Dallas, TX 75261-9911
Tel: 800-798-1822
http://www.acep.org

For industry information, contact
Association of Emergency Physicians
911 Whitewater Drive
Mars, PA 16046-4221
Tel: 866-772-1818
E-mail: aep@aep.org
http://www.aep.org

For information on residency training and careers, contact
Emergency Medicine Residents' Association
1125 Executive Circle
Irving, TX 75038-2522
Tel: 972-550-0920
http://www.emra.org

For information on emergency medical education, contact
Society for Academic Emergency Medicine
2340 South River Road, Suite 200
Des Plaines, IL 60018-3223
Tel: 847-813-9823
E-mail: saem@saem.org
http://www.saem.org/saemdnn

INTERVIEW

Dr. Joseph Cortez is an emergency medicine physician at Munster Community Hospital in Munster, Indiana. He discussed his career with the editors of Careers in Focus: Physicians.

Q. What made you want to enter this career?

A. The emergency medicine specialty is a perfect fit for me because I get to treat a wide variety of patients and their conditions. I currently see about 30 patients during a routine 10-hour shift.

Q. What are some of the pros and cons of your job?

A. Pros:
- You get the opportunity to interact with a variety of people.
- You can help people and save lives.
- When your shift ends your work is done, you're not "on call."
- Since you work in a hospital setting, there is no overhead cost associated with a clinic or private practice.

Cons:
- Work is very stressful; you are never sure what case is about to come into the emergency room (ER).
- Some days may be extremely busy, so you have to juggle multiple patients at a time, each requiring different forms of treatment.
- It's always hard to present family members with a difficult diagnosis or news of the death of a loved one.
- Shift work is assigned for different hours, and usually differs from week to week. Sometime you are given a morning shift, or afternoon, or overnight. It can be very taxing to your body clock!

Q. What advice would you give to young people who are interested in becoming emergency room physicians?

A. I would suggest interested students volunteer in the emergency room of your hospital. If volunteer positions are not available, consider shadowing an employee in the ER. Students should be prepared to study hard and get good grades. It's also important to note that studying is not done after one graduates from medical school. I have been in practice for more than 10 years, and I am still required to keep up with new medical procedures and developments in the field.

Endocrinologists

OVERVIEW

Endocrinologists are medical doctors who specialize in treatment of disorders of the endocrine system. The endocrine system is a network of glands in the body that secrete hormones into the bloodstream. Among other things, hormones control growth, reproduction, metabolism, and blood sugar levels. Thus, endocrinologists treat a wide variety of conditions. Although endocrinologists may be nurses, physiologists, and educators (to name just a few), this article will focus on endocrinologists as a physician specialty.

HISTORY

The study of endocrinology is often traced to the work of Charles-Edouard Brown-Sequard, a 19th-century French-American physiologist best known for his investigations of the nervous system. In 1889, Brown-Sequard began to experiment with an elixir containing an extract from guinea pig and dog testes. He claimed that the extract had rejuvenating effects, including increased stamina and strength. Although Brown-Sequard was largely ridiculed at the time, his elixir study provided an early understanding of the nature of testosterone, the hormone that leads to the development of male secondary sex characteristics.

The term *hormone* was first used by scientists Ernest Starling and William Bayliss in 1902, when they discovered secretin, the hormone that stimulates pancreatic secretion. The scientists went on to define a hormone as a chemical that is produced by an organ, is released in small amounts into the bloodstream, and is then transported to another organ to perform a specific task.

QUICK FACTS

School Subjects
Biology
Health

Personal Skills
Helping/teaching
Technical/scientific

Work Environment
Primarily indoors
Primarily multiple locations

Minimum Education Level
Medical degree

Salary Range
$120,000 to $170,102 to $221,633

Certification or Licensing
Required for certain positions (certification)
Required by all states (licensing)

Outlook
Much faster than the average

DOT
070

GOE
14.02.01

NOC
3112

O*NET-SOC
29-1063.00, 29-1067.00

Throughout the 20th century, scientific understanding of the endocrine system and hormones developed at a rapid pace. Today, the term *endocrinology* encompasses a broad range of scientific and medical studies.

THE JOB

From the pea-sized pituitary gland (which controls growth) to the adrenal glands (which respond to and regulate stress in the body), the endocrine system is part of the body's checks-and-balances system, regulating some of its most essential functions. When the body has trouble controlling hormone levels, an individual can suffer from a variety of problems, including thyroid disease, infertility, cholesterol disorders, glandular cancers, and diabetes, to name just a few. Disorders of the endocrine system are as varied and complex as glands and hormones themselves.

Endocrinologists are trained to help patients maintain the natural balance of hormones in their bodies. After diagnosing a patient, an endocrinologist might prescribe a hormone supplement or other medication; recommend changes to a patient's diet, exercise, or other habits; or refer the patient to specialists for other types of medical treatments, including surgery. Most endocrinologists are internists, obstetricians/gynecologists, or pediatricians who have completed a residency and fellowship in endocrinology. *Pediatric endocrinologists* treat disorders in growth and sexual development, as well as diseases such as diabetes and hypo- and hyperthyroidism. Pediatric endocrinologists work with patients ranging in age from infancy to adolescence. *Reproductive endocrinologists* treat patients dealing with conditions such as infertility, impotence, and problems related to menstruation and menopause. Some other areas of endocrinology specialization are diabetes, hypertension, weight disorders, and certain types of glandular cancers.

Endocrinology is a laboratory-oriented medical specialty, meaning that the diagnosis and treatment of endocrine disorders is heavily dependent on laboratory testing. Endocrinologists must have a firm understanding of the latest clinical research as well as the chemistry and biochemistry involved in laboratory tests. Endocrinologists must also be able to distinguish disease from human variation. For example, an endocrinologist may have to determine whether or not a child of below-average height is suffering from a hormonal imbalance.

As is the case with other types of physicians, endocrinologists' work is built around patient care. Endocrine disorders are often lifelong conditions, so endocrinologists form longstanding relationships with many patients as they manage their treatment.

REQUIREMENTS

High School

You can prepare for a career in endocrinology by taking courses in laboratory sciences such as biology, chemistry, and physics. Courses in algebra, trigonometry, geometry, and computer science will also be crucial for future laboratory work. Courses in English and speech will foster good communication skills, and classes in art and music will help broaden your understanding of the therapeutic nature of creative work.

Postsecondary Training

Endocrinologists must complete a bachelor's degree, usually in biology, chemistry, or a premed program. They then must earn a medical (M.D. or D.O.) degree (see "Physicians" and "Osteopathic Physicians"), which requires four years of medical school. For the first two years students attend lectures and classes and spend time in laboratories. They learn to take patient histories, perform routine physical examinations, and recognize symptoms. In the third and fourth years, they are involved in more practical studies. They work in clinics and hospitals supervised by residents and physicians and learn acute, chronic, preventive, and rehabilitative care. They go through what are known as rotations, or brief periods of study in a particular area, such as internal medicine, obstetrics and gynecology, pediatrics, psychiatry, and surgery. Then they must complete a minimum of four years in residency.

After completing a residency in internal medicine, obstetrics and gynecology, or pediatrics, a specialist in endocrinology must pursue a specialized internship or fellowship in the field, usually lasting an additional three to four years. The Association of Program Directors in Endocrinology, Diabetes, and Metabolism offers a list of fellowship programs at its Web site, http://www.apdem.org/programs. A list of fellowships can also be found at the Society for Reproductive Endocrinology and Infertility's http://www.socrei.org/FellowshipGateway.html.

Certification or Licensing

The American Board of Internal Medicine offers certification in endocrinology to those who complete training and licensing requirements. The American College of Endocrinology offers the Endocrine Certification in Neck Ultrasound to those who pass an examination. The American Board of Obstetrics and Gynecology offers subspecialty certification in endocrinology/infertility. Contact these organizations for more information.

All 50 states require physicians be licensed to practice. After graduating from medical school, you need to pass the licensing examination administered through the board of medical examiners in the state where you plan to practice.

Other Requirements

Communication skills are essential, as most of an endocrinologist's time is spent with patients, talking to them and listening to their histories and problems. Endocrinologists should be highly inquisitive and patient by nature, as this medical discipline relies heavily on laboratory testing and experimentation.

EARNINGS

First-year medical interns earned $47,458 in 2009, according to the Association of American Medical Colleges. Average starting salaries for endocrinologists range from $120,000 to $180,000, according to Physicians Search, a physician recruitment agency. Endocrinologists who have practiced for three years or more earn salaries that range from $123,984 to $221,633, with an average salary of $170,102.

Endocrinologists who work for hospitals, fertility clinics, and other employers usually receive benefits such as vacation days, sick leave, health and life insurance, and a savings and pension program. Self-employed endocrinologists must provide their own benefits.

OUTLOOK

According to the *Occupational Outlook Handbook*, the employment of physicians in all fields is expected to grow much faster than the average for all occupations through 2018. Endocrinologists are more frequently becoming the primary care physicians of patients with lifelong disorders such as diabetes and thyroid conditions. Since many of these conditions are on the rise as a result of an aging population and other societal trends, endocrinologists should be in strong demand in the coming decade.

FOR MORE INFORMATION

For news on endocrinology and for copies of professional journals, contact
American Association of Clinical Endocrinologists
245 Riverside Avenue, Suite 200
Jacksonville, FL 32202-4933
Tel: 904-353-7878
http://www.aace.com

For information about the career of endocrine surgeon, contact
American Association of Endocrine Surgeons
5810 West 140th Terrace
Overland Park, KS 66223-4201
Tel: 913-402-7102
E-mail: information@endocrinesurgery.org
http://www.endocrinesurgery.org

For information on certification, contact
American Board of Internal Medicine
510 Walnut Street, Suite 1700
Philadelphia, PA 19106-3699
Tel: 800-441-2246
http://www.abim.org

For information on certification, contact
American Board of Obstetrics and Gynecology
2915 Vine Street
Dallas, TX 75204-1045
Tel: 214-871-1619
http://www.abog.org

For information on board certification, contact
American College of Endocrinology
245 Riverside Avenue, Suite 200
Jacksonville, FL 32202-4933
Tel: 904-353-7878
http://www.aace.com/college

For information about endocrinology, contact
The Endocrine Society
8401 Connecticut Avenue, Suite 900
Chevy Chase, MD 20815-5817
Tel: 301-941-0200
http://www.endo-society.org

For information on fellowships, contact
Society for Reproductive Endocrinology and Infertility
E-mail: asrm@asrm.org
http://www.socrei.org

For career resources, contact
Women in Endocrinology
http://www.women-in-endo.org

Epidemiologists

QUICK FACTS

School Subjects
Biology
Health

Personal Skills
Helping/teaching
Technical/scientific

Work Environment
Primarily indoors
Primarily multiple locations

Minimum Education Level
Master's degree

Salary Range
$40,860 to $61,700 to
$92,610+

Certification or Licensing
Required for certain
positions (certification)
Required by all states
(licensing for physicians)

Outlook
Faster than the average

DOT
2161, 3114

GOE
02.03.01

NOC
N/A

O*NET-SOC
19-1041.00

OVERVIEW

Epidemiologists study the cause, spread, and control of diseases affecting groups of people or communities. They use statistics, research, and field investigations to try to connect incidences of a disease with characteristics of populations and communities. Some epidemiologists focus on infectious diseases, which are caused by bacteria and viruses and include AIDS, chicken pox, rabies, and meningitis. Others focus on noninfectious diseases including heart disease, lung cancer, breast cancer, and ulcers. Approximately 4,800 epidemiologists are employed in the United States.

HISTORY

Epidemiology is the study of diseases that affect large numbers of people. This branch of medical science did not become possible until the 1800s, when statistical analysis were applied to the understanding of disease. There are some signs, however, that earlier civilizations were making connections between disease and environmental factors. Early Hippocratic writings connect specific diseases to locations, seasons, and climates. In 1865, Louis Pasteur showed that a specific organism was causing an epidemic in silkworms. Robert Koch, a German bacteriologist, established the bacterial cause of tuberculosis in humans in 1882.

Toward the mid-1900s, chronic disease epidemiology began, focusing on the rise in peptic ulcer disease, coronary heart disease, and lung cancer. Chronic disease epidemiologists have helped show the links between smoking and lung cancer.

An epidemiologist (*right*) and a Virginia public health official speak at a press conference about an outbreak of swine flu cases in their state. (*Bob Brown, AP Photo*/Richmond Times-Dispatch)

Today, epidemiologists are increasingly interested in global health patterns and in applying new computer technology to the field.

THE JOB

Epidemiologists use research, statistical analysis, field investigations, and laboratory techniques to attempt to determine the cause of a disease, how it spreads, and what can be done to prevent and control it. They measure the incidence of a disease and relate it to characteristics of populations and environments. Many work on developing new methods or refining old ways of measuring and evaluating incidence of disease.

Epidemiologists' work is important to the medical community and to public health officials, who use their information to determine public health policies. Epidemiologists often develop and recommend public health policies using the research they have collected.

The field of epidemiology is complex, with multiple specializations. *Infectious disease epidemiologists* focus on diseases caused by bacteria and viruses, such as botulism and chicken pox. *Chronic disease epidemiologists* study noninfectious diseases that can be genetic or lifestyle-induced, such as lung cancer, heart disease, and ulcers.

Did You Know?

- Infectious diseases are the third leading cause of death in the United States.

- Infectious diseases are the second leading cause of death in the world.

- More than 40,000 people in the United States are diagnosed with HIV/AIDS each year.

- In the United States, health care associated infections account for two million infections and 90,000 deaths annually.

Source: Infectious Diseases Society of America

Some epidemiologists have done work on rising teenage suicide rates and murders by guns because they are considered epidemics.

Environmental epidemiologists study connections between environmental exposure and disease. They have linked radon with lung cancer, found that interior house paint can cause lead poisoning in children, and discovered that dust from soybeans caused an asthma epidemic in Barcelona, Spain.

Each state has its own head epidemiologist, who is usually part of the state's public health service. These state epidemiologists work closely with the U.S. Centers for Disease Control and Prevention (CDC) in Atlanta. States are required by law to report certain diseases in their populations to the CDC on a regular basis. For example, states must report outbreaks of influenza or incidences of food poisoning to the CDC.

REQUIREMENTS

High School
Classes such as biology, health, English, physics, and math (including statistics) are recommended. Social studies and geography also are relevant. In addition, take the opportunity to develop your computer skills because epidemiology increasingly makes use of the latest information technology.

Postsecondary Training
A four-year bachelor of science degree is the minimum requirement to enter an epidemiology program. You will need at least a master's

degree in public health to work as an epidemiologist. Some employers require epidemiologists to have a Ph.D. or a medical degree. For example, epidemiologists who work at health care facilities and hospitals often must have a medical degree and training in infectious diseases. Epidemiologists also need to complete some postdoctoral training such as a fellowship.

Certification or Licensing
The Certification Board of Infection Control and Epidemiology, a subgroup of the Association for Professionals in Infection Control and Epidemiology, offers certification to epidemiology professionals. Contact the board for more information.

All physicians in the United States must be licensed to practice. Some states have reciprocity agreements with other states so that a physician licensed in one state may be automatically licensed in another without being required to pass another examination.

Other Requirements
Epidemiologists need to be good scientists and statisticians. They also need to be skilled with computers and like helping people. Curiosity, determination, persistence, and drive will help in research.

EXPLORING
To explore your interest in epidemiology, visit the Web site of the CDC (http://www.cdc.gov) to read about topics such as environmental health, vaccines and immunizations, and to read articles from the *Emerging Infectious Diseases* journal (http://www.cdc.gov/ncidod/EID). It would also be helpful to read about past epidemics and how they were dealt with. A recent example is the story of the polio epidemic of the 20th century and Jonas Salk's and Albert Sabin's race to find a vaccine against it. A good book on the topic is *Polio: An American Story*, by David M. Oshinsky (New York: Oxford University Press, USA, 2006).

EMPLOYERS
There are approximately 4,800 epidemiologists working in the United States, with a majority employed in government. Epidemiologists work for state public health services, local communities, and counties. The CDC employs many epidemiologists, too. Different branches of the CDC focus on different diseases or public health practices. Epidemiologists with the CDC may conduct research, help

states exchange information about disease control and prevention, and help make recommendations for public health policies.

Most environmental epidemiologists work for the federal government or in state public health departments. The biggest federal employer is the U.S. Department of Health and Human Services, primarily the CDC, the Agency for Toxic Substances and Disease Registry, and the National Institute of Environmental Health Sciences.

Some epidemiologists work for universities, where they teach and do research. Others work for the World Health Organization (WHO) and The AIDS Institute. Hospitals also employ epidemiologists, usually to research chronic or infectious diseases. Others work in the pharmaceutical industry and at scientific research and development firms.

STARTING OUT

After receiving at least a bachelor's degree, you would be eligible to start a graduate program in epidemiology. Many graduate students in these programs, however, have a medical degree. Typical programs are four years, but there are some two-year degree programs. During graduate school, you should start contacting employers about jobs.

ADVANCEMENT

Advancement in the field of epidemiology depends on your interest and where you are working. An epidemiologist teaching at a university could advance from assistant professor to full professor. Epidemiologists working for a state's head epidemiologist could move on to become the state epidemiologist there or in another state. Some epidemiologists might want to advance to international work.

EARNINGS

According to the U.S. Department of Labor (DOL), median annual earnings for epidemiologists were $61,700 in 2009, with the lowest paid 10 percent earning less than $40,860, and the highest paid 10 percent earning more than $92,610. The DOL reports the following mean annual salaries for epidemiologists by employer: scientific research and development services, $79,210; general medical and surgical hospitals, $76,030; and colleges, universities, and professional schools, $62,320.

Epidemiologists who work full time for government agencies and other employers receive benefits such as vacation days, sick leave, health and life insurance, and a savings and pension program. Self-employed epidemiologists must provide their own benefits.

WORK ENVIRONMENT

Depending on where epidemiologists work, part of their day might be spent in the office and part in the community. Most spend part of their time working in teams and part on their own. They may monitor the site of a disease, take samples, collect data, and check out any outbreaks among community residents. Back in the office, they might download their data, conduct research, analyze samples, and write reports.

OUTLOOK

Employment for epidemiologists is projected to grow faster than the average for all careers through 2018, according to the U.S. Department of Labor. Job prospects for epidemiologists are promising because there will always be a need to understand, control, and prevent the spread of disease. There is particular promise in the growing field of environmental epidemiology. Positions in epidemiology will be highly competitive, however, as the number of positions are limited.

The Centers for Disease Control and Prevention have only been in existence since 1946, and the World Health Organization since 1948. Less-developed countries still have high rates of tuberculosis, syphilis, malaria, and other diseases. Even developed countries experience periodic recurrences of infectious diseases; organisms that cause illness sometimes become resistant to existing vaccines. In addition, new strains of diseases are discovered all the time, such as Lyme disease in 1975, the Hantavirus in 1976, and Legionnaires' disease in 1977.

In 1993, the Cryptosporidium parasite tainted the water supply in Milwaukee, Wisconsin, and infected more than 400,000 people. Not long after, a strain of E. coli in undercooked meat made 300 people ill in the Northwest. In 1995, the Ebola virus, which causes massive hemorrhaging and terrible suffering in its victims, emerged in Africa for the first time in almost 20 years.

More recently, there has been great public concern over bovine spongiform encephalopathy, or BSE ("mad cow" disease); Creutzfeldt-Jakob disease, or CJD (foot-and-mouth disease); SARS;

necrotizing fasciitis ("flesh-eating" disease), and the H1N1 influenza virus. In addition, interest in preventing bioterrorism is of great importance.

Developments in technology will drive epidemiological research to improve the understanding and prevention of disease. Biomedical techniques such as genetic recombination and imaging are revolutionizing the field. The use of new information systems will make global communication more comprehensive and efficient among nations.

The need to understand the social context of disease transmission will also create opportunities for epidemiologists. Medical professionals may know what causes a disease and work to prevent its spread, but it is the epidemiologist's job to work on identifying and changing negative social behaviors to keep outbreaks from ever starting.

FOR MORE INFORMATION

For information on continuing education and certification, contact
Association for Professionals in Infection Control
    and Epidemiology
1275 K Street, NW, Suite 1000
Washington, DC 20005-4006
Tel: 202-789-1890
E-mail: apicinfo@apic.org
http://www.apic.org

For publications and training and employment opportunities, contact
Centers for Disease Control and Prevention
1600 Clifton Road, NE
Atlanta, GA 30333
Tel: 800-232-4636
E-mail: cdcinfo@cdc.gov
http://www.cdc.gov

For information on certification, contact
Certification Board of Infection Control and Epidemiology
555 East Wells Street, Suite 1100
Milwaukee, WI 53202-3800
Tel: 414-918-9796
E-mail: info@cbic.org
http://www.cbic.org

For information on public health epidemiology, contact
Council of State and Territorial Epidemiologists
2872 Woodcock Boulevard, Suite 303
Atlanta, GA 30341-4015
Tel: 770-458-3811
http://www.cste.org/dnn

For information on postgraduate training in epidemiology, contact
Epidemic Intelligence Service
Centers for Disease Control and Prevention
1600 Clifton Road, NE, Mailstop E-92
Atlanta, GA 30333
Tel: 404-498-6110
E-mail: EIS@cdc.gov
http://www.cdc.gov/eis

Visit the society's Web site for information on educational programs and to read A World of Opportunities: Career Paths in Infectious Diseases and HIV Medicine.
Infectious Diseases Society of America
1300 Wilson Boulevard, Suite 300
Arlington, VA 22209-2332
Tel: 703-299-0200
E-mail: info@idsociety.org
http://www.idsociety.org

Gastroenterologists

QUICK FACTS

School Subjects
Biology
Health

Personal Skills
Helping/teaching
Technical/scientific

Work Environment
Primarily indoors
Primarily multiple locations

Minimum Education Level
Medical degree

Salary Range
$100,000 to $280,000 to
$381,340+

Certification or Licensing
Required for certain
positions (certification)
Required by all states
(licensing)

Outlook
Much faster than the average

DOT
070

GOE
14.02.01

NOC
3112

O*NET-SOC
29-1069.00

OVERVIEW

Gastroenterologists are physicians who specialize in the treatment of the digestive system and associated organs, like the liver and gall bladder.

HISTORY

Gastroenterologists treat any disease of the digestive system, from chronic heartburn to cancer. The American College of Gastroenterology was founded in 1932. The study of the digestive system is as old as medicine, but in recent years there have been a number of important breakthroughs. Peptic ulcers, a common type of ulcer affecting millions of people, have been linked to the Heliobacter pylori bacteria. Through research, gastroenterologists learned that treating patients with antibiotics, along with the regular treatments given for ulcers, dramatically lowered recurrence of the disease. Other advances are technological in nature. Computers and fiber-optic technology have allowed gastroenterologists tremendous flexibility in the diagnosis and treatment of conditions that in the past would have required surgery.

THE JOB

Gastroenterologists are internal medicine physicians specializing in the treatment of the digestive system, including the small intestine, colon, rectum, stomach, pancreas, gall bladder, bile ducts, esophagus, and liver. They examine patients, prescribe drugs when needed, diagnose disease, and perform various procedures to treat those diseases.

Endoscopy and Fiber Optics

Endoscopy, one of the major diagnostic tools of gastroenterologists, enables doctors to actually see into their patients' bodies using fiber optics, which are made of thin and flexible glass, quartz, or plastic fibers that conduct light using internal reflection. An endoscope uses two fiber-optic lines, one of which transmits light and the other which carries the image back to the doctor's viewing lens or monitor. The first attempts to see into the body were made in the early 1900s with lighted telescopes. In the early 1930s, semiflexible gastroscopes were used to see inside the stomach. Fiber optics were developed in the 1950s, and physician Basil Hirschowitz became the first to use fiber optics for endoscopy.

Technological advances in gastroenterology have made the diagnosis and treatment of certain types of gastrointestinal problems much easier on the patient. One of these advances is endoscopy. An endoscope is a medical instrument that enables physicians to see organs and cavities in the body that are otherwise hidden from view. The endoscope is inserted through a natural opening, such as the mouth or rectum. It is a long thin tube with an optic viewing system that transmits images of the patient's body to a monitor. Endoscopy is a commonly use by gastroenterologists for such things as flexible sigmoidoscopy (view of rectum to lower colon), colonoscopy (view of the entire colon from rectum to lower end of the small intestine), upper GI endoscopy (view of the esophagus, stomach, duodenum), and ERCP (view of the liver, gallbladder, pancreas, bile ducts).

Patients who undergo colonoscopy are most likely adults over age 50. A diagnosis of colon cancer or colorectal polyps (benign growths that occur on the lining of the colon and rectum that can become cancerous) can be confirmed through colonoscopy. Patients who undergo colonoscopy have generally been referred by a family physician who has performed other less invasive tests and suspects polyps or cancer. Only a gastroenterologist can perform a colonoscopy. If the cells removed during the colonoscopy prove cancerous, a gastroenterologist or other specialist such as a colon and rectal surgeon will perform surgery to remove the cancerous polyps and other malignant tissue.

Colon and rectal surgeons are just one of the many specialists gastroenterologists work closely with in treating diseases of the digestive system. *Oncologists* (cancer specialists), *cardiologists* (heart specialists), and other surgeons may collaborate to ensure the best possible care. The chronic nature of many gastrointestinal problems means that doctors often have patients for years, building long-term relationships. Patients who suffer from gastrointestinal problems generally experience some level of discomfort from their symptoms, which can include heartburn, nausea, vomiting, diarrhea, and bloating. They are especially appreciative when a gastroenterologist can relieve symptoms that have severely limited their lifestyle and quality of life.

REQUIREMENTS

High School
Medical training requires a very strong background in the sciences, so you should take as many science classes as you can. Biology and chemistry are most important, but physics, anatomy, and others are also helpful. Mathematics and humanities, especially English, will help prepare you for the rigorous academic demands encountered in college and medical school.

Postsecondary Training
After completing medical school and becoming licensed to practice medicine (see "Physicians" and "Osteopathic Physicians"), prospective gastroenterologists enter an internal medicine residency that lasts three years. Following residency, they spend an additional two to three years in a gastroenterology fellowship. Competition for these available openings is fierce.

Certification or Licensing
To become board certified as a gastroenterologist, individuals must first become certified in internal medicine by the American Board of Internal Medicine. Requirements for internal medicine certification include graduation from an accredited medical school, three years of postdoctoral training, proven clinical competency, and passage of a comprehensive examination. Additional requirements for certification in the subspecialty of gastroenterology include three years of training in gastroenterology, 18 months of clinical practice, and passing a comprehensive subspecialty exam.

All 50 states require physicians be licensed to practice. After graduating from medical school, you need to pass the licensing examination administered through the board of medical examiners in the state where you plan to practice.

Other Requirements

Gastroenterologists must be able to communicate effectively with other health care professionals and with patients. This includes being a keen listener. A large part of successful treatment is accurate diagnosis, which requires carefully taken patient histories and close analysis of symptoms. Gastroenterologists must also be able to work with all types of people and have a deep sense of caring and compassion.

EARNINGS

First-year interns earned $47,458 in 2009, according to the Association of American Medical Colleges. The U.S. Department of Labor reports that doctors specializing in internal medicine earned mean annual salaries of $183,990 in 2009. Salaries for gastroenterologists in their first year of practice ranged from $100,000 to $280,000, according to Physicians Search, a physician recruitment agency. Those in practice for three years or longer reported earnings of $179,000 to $381,340 with a median of $292,133 annually.

In general, self-employed gastroenterologists who own their own medical practice had higher incomes than salaried physicians hired by a hospital or medical group. Salary levels are also affected by experience, geographic region, hours worked, and professional reputation.

Gastroenterologists who are employed by hospitals and other medical organizations usually receive benefits such as vacation days, sick leave, health and life insurance, and a savings and pension program. Gastroenterologists who operate their own practices must provide their own benefits.

OUTLOOK

The U.S. Department of Labor predicts that employment for physicians will grow much faster than the average for all careers through 2018. If the current trend continues, the outlook for gastroenterologists and other medical specialists looks especially bright. The current growing demand for specialty care (particularly by a growing aging population) coupled with a shortage of trained physicians has resulted in a good job market for those who choose to specialize.

FOR MORE INFORMATION

For information on certification requirements, contact
American Board of Internal Medicine
510 Walnut Street, Suite 1700
Philadelphia, PA 19106-3699
Tel: 800-441-2246
http://www.abim.org

For information on gastrointestinal disorders, contact
American College of Gastroenterology
PO Box 342260
Bethesda, MD 20827-2260
Tel: 301-263-9000
http://www.acg.gi.org

For information on careers and training programs, contact
American Gastroenterological Association
4930 Del Ray Avenue
Bethesda, MD 20814-2512
Tel: 301-654-2055
E-mail: member@gastro.org
http://www.gastro.org

General Practitioners

OVERVIEW

General practitioners (GPs), sometimes referred to as *family practice physicians* or *family practitioners*, are primary care physicians. They are usually the first health care professional patients consult. They treat people of all ages and tend to see the same patients on a continuing basis, often for years. General practitioners diagnose and treat any illness or injury that does not require the service of a specialist. They frequently serve as the family doctor, treating all the members of a family. There are approximately 99,000 general practitioners employed in the United States.

HISTORY

While "family doctors" or the "general doc" have been a part of the health care picture ever since medicine began, today's efforts to control health care costs have led insurance companies to the increased use of Health Maintenance Organizations (HMOs) and Preferred Provider Organizations (PPOs). These plans often limit the use of specialists, making subscribers seek care first from a primary care physician. Because of this, patients who might once have gone directly to a specialist without seeing a general practitioner must now see their general practitioner first in order to get a referral to see a specialist.

THE JOB

The general practitioner sees patients ranging in age from newborns to the elderly. Unlike a specialist, the GP treats the whole patient, not just a specific illness or body system. The general practitioner may give the patient diet and lifestyle advice, as well as methods for preventing disease or injury. Some general practitioners may also provide prenatal care and deliver babies. The GP treats patients who have a wide variety of ailments and orders diagnostic tests and procedures, if necessary. If a patient comes in with an illness that

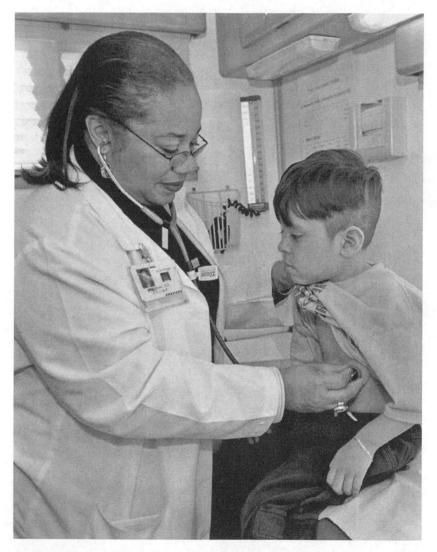

A general practitioner examines a boy inside a medical mobile unit that offers residents of homeless shelters free medical services. *(Monika Graff, The Image Works)*

requires special medical treatment, that patient is often referred to an appropriate specialist.

The general practitioner usually works with a staff of nurses and office personnel. Other physicians and medical personnel may be a part of the office setup as well.

Usually about 70 percent of a general practitioner's workday is spent seeing patients in an office. They also treat patients in hospitals, confer with other medical personnel, patients, and family members, and perform limited surgery. Some practitioners might make house calls if the patient is unable to come to the office. In some private office situations, the general practitioner also oversees the office finances, equipment and supply purchases, and personnel. Many general practitioners must be on call to treat patients after regular office hours. If the GP works in a medical group they usually take turns being on call. General practitioners work long, irregular hours. According to the American Academy of Family Physicians, general practitioners averaged nearly 51 hours per week in 2008. Physicians in solo or private practice put in more hours, on average, than physicians who were employed by managed care facilities.

REQUIREMENTS

High School
High school students who plan to become physicians should take a college preparatory curriculum that includes history, social studies, math, and foreign languages. Specific high school classes that will be helpful to prospective physicians include biology, chemistry, physics, and physiology. English and speech classes are also useful because doctors need to develop good communication skills, both written and oral.

Postsecondary Training
After receiving the doctor of medicine (M.D.) or the doctor of osteopathic medicine (D.O.) degree, you must fulfill a one- to three-year hospital residency requirement where you are actively involved in patient treatment as part of a hospital medical team. At the end of an accredited residency program, physicians must pass certification examinations. (See the articles "Osteopaths" and "Physicians" for more information on the specifics of medical school.)

Certification or Licensing
Board certification is granted by the American Board of Family Medicine. This credential, though voluntary, signifies that the physician is highly qualified in family practice. To be eligible to

take the credentialing exam, applicants must have satisfactorily completed three years of residency training accredited by the Accreditation Council for Graduate Medical Education (http://www.acgme.org) after receiving their medical degree from an accredited institution.

All states and the District of Columbia require physicians to be licensed. General practitioners seeking licensure must graduate from an accredited medical school, complete residency postgraduate training, and pass a licensing examination administered by their state's board of medical examiners. Some states have reciprocity agreements so that a physician licensed to practice in one state may be automatically licensed in another state without having to pass another examination.

Other Requirements

To be a successful general practitioner, you should be committed to helping people, and be compassionate and understanding. You should have good communication skills to communicate with other staff members, patients, and their families, and be able to inspire their confidence and trust. In addition, a GP should have the stamina to work long and irregular hours.

EXPLORING

As with any career, talking with a high school counselor and interviewing those working in the field are useful ways to explore your interest. You might also want to read professional magazines—such as *American Family Physician, Family Practice Management,* and *Annals of Family Medicine*—to learn more about business and practice issues affecting general practitioners. Sample articles from these publications can be accessed at the American Academy of Family Physicians Web site, http://www.aafp.org. The Web site also provides a wealth of information and statistics about the career.

Volunteering at local hospitals or at other health care facilities will help you gain exposure to a medical environment and experience helping people, even if your job involves delivering flowers or filling water pitchers in patients' rooms.

EMPLOYERS

Approximately 99,000 general practitioners are employed in the United States. General practitioners may choose to open a solo private practice, join a partnership or group practice, or take a salaried job in a clinic or managed care (HMO or PPO) network. Salaried positions are also available with federal and state agencies, neighborhood health centers, and the military, including the Department of Veterans Affairs. Other physicians may decide to teach at medical schools or university hospitals.

The majority of physicians practice in urban areas, near hospitals and educational centers. Therefore, competition for patients is likely to be higher in these areas. In contrast, rural communities and small towns are often in need of doctors and may be promising places for young physicians to establish practices.

STARTING OUT

Many new physicians choose to join existing practices instead of attempting to start their own. Establishing a new practice is costly, and it may take time to build a patient base. In a clinic, group practice, or partnership, physicians share the costs for medical equipment and staff salaries, as well as establish a wider patient base.

General practitioners who hope to join an existing practice may find leads through their medical school or residency. During these experiences, they work with many members of the medical community, some of which may be able to recommend them to appropriate practices.

Another approach would be to check the various medical professional journals, which often run ads for physician positions. Aspiring physicians can also hire a medical placement agency to assist them in the job search.

Physicians who hope to work for a managed care organization or government sponsored clinic should contact the source directly for information on position availability and application procedures.

ADVANCEMENT

There are few advancement possibilities for general practitioners. Like most other physicians, these doctors stay in their field, building their practices until retirement. As they build their patient bases and reputations, their practices become larger and their incomes steadily increase. For those who work in a large group practice, advancement may come in the form of opening a private practice.

Some general practitioners decide to pursue a teaching or research career at a college or university. Generally, these doctors first earn a Ph.D. in the sciences.

EARNINGS

Physicians, as a group, have among the highest annual earnings of all occupations. The mean annual income for general practitioners was $168,550 in 2009, according to the U.S. Department of Labor. The lowest paid 10 percent earned $82,630 or less annually; the highest paid 10 percent earned more than $192,330. General practitioners with established patient bases and reputations can earn more than $200,000 a year.

Those affiliated with a group practice generally make more than those in solo practice and those who are self-employed may earn considerably more than salaried employees do. A general practitioner's income may be affected by years of experience and tends to peak between the ages of 56 and 65.

Physicians who are self-employed must provide their own insurance coverage. Those who are employed by an HMO, clinic, or other organization may receive a benefits package including insurance and paid time off.

WORK ENVIRONMENT

The offices and examining rooms of general practitioners are well equipped, attractive, well lighted, and well ventilated. There are usually several nurses, a laboratory technician, one or more secretaries, a bookkeeper, and a receptionist available to assist the GP. General practitioners usually see patients by appointments that are scheduled according to individual requirements. They may reserve all mornings for hospital visits and minor surgery. They may see patients in the office only on certain days of the week. General practitioners may also visit patients in nursing homes, hospices, and home care settings.

OUTLOOK

Employment of physicians is expected to grow much faster than the average for all occupations through 2018, according to the U.S. Department of Labor. One reason for growth is that the population is steadily increasing and people are living longer, requiring more health care services.

Job prospects are especially good for primary care physicians because more insurance companies are using HMOs and PPOs. These plans require that their insurance holders see a general practitioner first in order to get a referral to a specialist.

Because most physicians choose to practice in urban areas, these areas are often oversupplied and fiercely competitive. General practitioners just entering the field may find it difficult to enter a practice and build a patient base in a big city. Because of this oversupply, future physicians may be more likely to work fewer hours, have lower earnings, or practice in underserved areas. There is a growing need for physicians in rural communities and small towns, so general practitioners who are willing to relocate to these areas should have excellent job prospects.

FOR MORE INFORMATION

For information on the career of general practitioner, contact
American Academy of Family Physicians
PO Box 11210
Shawnee Mission, KS 66207-1210
Tel: 800-274-2237
E-mail: contactcenter@aafp.org
http://www.aafp.org

To read the Osteopathic Medical College Information Book and for information on financial aid, visit the Web site of the AACOM.
American Association of Colleges of Osteopathic Medicine (AACOM)
5550 Friendship Boulevard, Suite 310
Chevy Chase, MD 20815-7231
Tel: 301-968-4100
http://www.aacom.org

For information on board certification, contact
American Board of Family Medicine
1648 McGrathiana Parkway, Suite 550
Lexington, KY 40511-1247
Tel: 888-995-5700
E-mail: help@theabfm.org
https://www.theabfm.org

For general information about careers in medicine, contact
American Medical Association
515 North State Street
Chicago, IL 60654-4854
Tel: 800-621-8335
http://www.ama-assn.org

For information on osteopathic medicine, contact
American Osteopathic Association
142 East Ontario Street
Chicago, IL 60611-2874
Tel: 800-621-1773
http://www.osteopathic.org

To learn more about medical education, contact
Association of American Medical Colleges
2450 N Street, NW
Washington, DC 20037-1126
Tel: 202-828-0400
http://www.aamc.org

Geriatricians

OVERVIEW

A *geriatrician* is a physician with specialized knowledge in the prevention, diagnosis, treatment, and rehabilitation of disorders common to old age. The term *geriatrics* refers to the clinical aspects of aging and the comprehensive health care of older people. It is an area of medicine that focuses on health and disease in old age and is a growing medical specialty.

HISTORY

Geriatricians specialize in working with the elderly. The term geriatrics comes from the Greek terms, *geras*, meaning old age, and *iatrikos*, meaning physician. Geriatrics has only fairly recently become a popular, necessary, and recognized specialty. Formal training in the field is relatively new. One reason for the development of this occupation is that people are now living longer. According to the U.S. Census Bureau, there were three million Americans age 65 or over living in 1900, but by 1999 this segment of the population had grown to about 35 million. This large (and growing) number of older people has created a demand for specialized services. Geriatricians are doctors who fulfill this demand. As our elderly population continues to grow—the bureau predicts approximately 82 million people to be age 65 or over by 2050—geriatricians are faced with unique medical and ethical challenges in the treatment of their patients.

THE JOB

Geriatricians spend most of their time with patients, taking patient histories, listening to their comments or symptoms, and running any of a number of diagnostic tests and evaluations, including physical examinations. Geriatricians generally see patients in a clinic, a long-term care facility, or a hospital. Each patient setting requires a unique type of patient care. Geriatricians often work with other physicians to diagnose and treat multiple problems and to provide the best possible care for each patient.

For example, an elderly man's complaint of fatigue could signal one or more of a large number of disorders. Diagnosis may be complicated by the coexistence of physical and mental problems, such as heart disease and dementia (mental confusion). This may mean consulting with a psychiatrist to treat the dementia and a cardiologist for the heart problems. Not only do geriatricians work with other medical personnel, they also work with family members and community services. Very often, geriatricians work with the patient's family in order to get an accurate diagnosis, proper care, and follow-up treatment. If the patient is living alone, the geriatrician might also need the support of a social worker, neighbor, or relative to make certain that proper medication is administered and that the patient is monitored. If there is no cure for the patient's condition, the geriatrician must devise some way of helping the patient cope with the condition.

Paperwork is also a large part of geriatricians' jobs, as they must complete forms, sign releases, write prescriptions, and meet the requirements of Medicare and private insurance companies.

REQUIREMENTS

High School

To become a doctor, you will need to devote many years to schooling before you are admitted to practice. Your first step, therefore, should be to take a college preparatory curriculum while in high school. Take four years of math, English, and science classes. Biology, chemistry, and physics are particularly important to take. Study a foreign language and, if your high school offers it, the language you take should be Latin. Many medical terms you will encounter later on have roots in the Latin language. In addition, round out your education with history courses and courses such as psychology and sociology, which may give you a greater understanding of people, an asset in this people-oriented career.

Facts About Geriatric Populations

- Although people over the age of 65 make up only 12 percent of the U.S. population, this group requires nearly 40 percent of all surgical procedures.

- By 2050, 20.6 percent of Americans will be age 65 or older—an increase of nearly 8 percent from 2004.

- Twenty percent of Medicare patients have at least five chronic conditions such as diabetes, arthritis, and hypertension. Geriatricians receive special training to diagnose and treat these conditions in the elderly.

Source: American Geriatrics Society, Centers for Disease Control and Prevention

Postsecondary Training

To become a geriatrician, you will need to earn a college degree and a medical degree, complete specialized training, and become licensed. (See "Physicians" and "Osteopathic Physicians.") After students have completed this phase of their education, they get more training through a residency, with study in a specialty area. Geriatric care is generally considered a subspecialty. So students complete their residency in one specialty area, such as internal medicine, and then go on to complete a fellowship in geriatric care. The length of these programs varies, and they can take anywhere from one to four years to complete. The Association for Gerontology in Higher Education publishes the *Directory of Educational Programs in Gerontology and Geriatrics*, which has information on educational programs available at various levels, including fellowship programs.

Certification or Licensing

A certificate of added qualifications in geriatric medicine or geriatric psychiatry is offered through the certifying boards in family practice, internal medicine, osteopathic medicine, and psychiatry for physicians who have completed a fellowship program in geriatrics. The American Board of Internal Medicine is just one of many professional medical boards that provide certification to qualified geriatricians.

In addition, all physicians must be licensed to practice. After receiving their medical degree, new physicians are required to take a licensing examination conducted through the board of medical examiners in each state. Some states have reciprocity agreements with other states so that a physician licensed in one state may be automatically licensed in another without being required to pass another examination. Because this is not true throughout the United States, however, the wise physician will find out about licensing procedures before planning to move.

Other Requirements

The career of a geriatrician is both intellectually and emotionally demanding. A good geriatrician needs to be able to effectively manage all aspects of a patient's problems, including social and emotional issues. Thus, creative problem-solving skills are an asset. Geriatricians must have a general interest in aging and the problems related to growing older. They should be effective communicators and listeners and be able to work well as members of a team. And, like any doctor, geriatricians must be committed to lifelong learning, because new advances in medicine occur continuously.

EARNINGS

First-year medical interns earned $47,458 in 2009, according to the Association of American Medical Colleges. According to a salary survey conducted by the recruiting agency Physicians Search, starting salaries for those in internal medicine range from approximately $100,000 to $280,000. The mean salary for those specializing in internal medicine was $183,990 in 2009, according to the U.S. Department of Labor (DOL). The DOL reports that salaries for all physicians ranged from $51,750 to more than $205,970. Although these are not figures specifically for geriatricians, they are comparable to what these specialists earn. Earnings are also affected by what area of the country a physician works in, type of employer, size of the practice, and even his or her reputation.

Benefits depend on the employer, but usually include standard ones such as vacation time and insurance. Self-employed geriatricians must provide their own benefits.

OUTLOOK

Employment for all physicians is expected to grow much faster than the average for all careers through 2018. The outlook should be even better for those working in geriatric medicine. As the large generation of baby boomers ages, more physicians will be needed to treat their specific needs. Only a small number of physicians each year decide to work in geriatrics. The American Geriatrics Society reports that there is currently a shortage of geriatricians. There is currently only one geriatrician for every 5,000 adults who are age 65 and older. If expected shortages continue, there will only be one geriatrician for every 7,665 older adults by 2030—which suggests that employment opportunities will be especially strong for workers in this field.

FOR MORE INFORMATION

For information on geriatric psychiatry, contact
American Association for Geriatric Psychiatry
7910 Woodmont Avenue, Suite 1050
Bethesda, MD 20814-3004
Tel: 301-654-7850
E-mail: main@aagponline.org
http://www.aagpgpa.org

For information on board certification, contact
American Board of Family Medicine
1648 McGrathiana Parkway, Suite 550
Lexington, KY 40511-1247
Tel: 888-995-5700
E-mail: help@theabfm.org
https://www.theabfm.org

For general information on geriatric care, contact
The American Geriatrics Society
350 Fifth Avenue, Suite 801
New York, NY 10118-0801
Tel: 212-308-1414
E-mail: info@americangeriatrics.org
http://www.americangeriatrics.org

For information on careers in aging, visit the following Web site:
Association for Gerontology in Higher Education
1220 L Street, NW, Suite 901
Washington, DC 20005-4018
Tel: 202-289-9806http://www.aghe.org

Visit the following Web site for detailed information about careers in gerontology:
Careers in Aging: Resources for Developing Your Career in Aging
http://www.aghe.org/templates/System/details.asp?id=40634
&PID=500215

Hematologists

QUICK FACTS

School Subjects
Biology
Chemistry

Personal Skills
Helping/teaching
Technical/scientific

Work Environment
Primarily indoors
Primarily multiple locations

Minimum Education Level
Doctorate

Salary Range
$120,000 to $269,298 to
$473,000

Certification or Licensing
Required for certain positions (certification)
Required by all states (for M.D.s) (licensing)

Outlook
Faster than the average

DOT
070

GOE
14.02.01

NOC
3111

O*NET-SOC
29-1069.00

OVERVIEW

Hematologists study and/or treat diseases of the blood and the blood-forming tissues. Some hematologists are physicians (M.D.s) who specialize in blood diseases; other hematologists are medical scientists (Ph.D.'s) who do research on blood diseases but do not treat patients. A few students who plan to focus on medical research choose to do a joint M.D./Ph.D. program.

HISTORY

Hematology is classified as a subspecialty of internal medicine, the branch of medicine that studies and treats, usually by nonsurgical means, diseases of the body's internal organs. This exciting, high-tech field in medical research has made dramatic advances in recent decades. Many forms of leukemia that would formerly have caused death within a few months of diagnosis are now curable because of research performed by hematologists.

In 1958, the American Society of Hematology was founded to represent the professional interests of hematologists.

THE JOB

Some hematologists are medical scientists who do blood-related research but do not treat patients. Others are physicians who have chosen to specialize in blood diseases and their treatment. Some physicians in hematology work with patients, while others are more research oriented and work primarily in research laboratories.

The duties of a hematologist depend on whether the hematologist is a research scientist or a medical doctor. In the case of a doctor, it

Learn More About It

Visit the following Web sites for more information on blood and hematology:

BloodLine
http://www.bloodline.net

The Bloody Bits
http://www.blood.co.uk/funzone/bloodybits/

Facts About Blood
http://www.umm.edu/blood/blood.htm

Introduction to Hematology
http://www.psbc.org/hematology

My Blood, Your Blood
http://www.mybloodyourblood.org

Red Gold: The Epic Story of Blood
http://www.pbs.org/wnet/redgold

also depends on whether he or she is primarily involved in research or in patient treatment. As a subspecialty of internal medicine, hematology is also closely connected with oncology, the internal medicine subspecialty dealing with tumors. Hematology and oncology are often combined into a single department in medical schools. Doctors who specialize in pediatric hematology-oncology work exclusively with children who have blood disorders and/or cancer.

Hematologists who work in academic research settings mainly conduct research, which also includes supervising the lab and the people who work in it, writing grants to get federal money to fund the lab, as well as other responsibilities, such as lecturing and teaching.

REQUIREMENTS

High School

Future scientists and physicians should take college prep courses in high school. Laboratory sciences (biology, chemistry, physics) and mathematics are especially important as the foundation for more advanced work later. English, foreign languages, history, and other humanities and social sciences courses are important as well. Good oral and written communication skills are essential.

Postsecondary Training

A premed program is best if you plan to go to medical school. If there is no premed program, or if you want to pursue a Ph.D. program, then chemistry or biology is an appropriate undergraduate major. Some colleges also offer undergraduate majors in biochemistry, microbiology, or genetics.

You must take the Medical College Admission Test (MCAT) before applying to medical school and the Graduate Record Exam (GRE) before applying to graduate school. Apply to at least three medical or graduate schools to increase your chances of acceptance.

Medical school and Ph.D. programs in the biomedical sciences generally take at least four years. A combined M.D./Ph.D. or D.O./Ph.D. program usually takes six to seven years.

After graduating from medical school, students spend at least three years in a hospital residency program. The length of the residency period depends on the specialty chosen. Because hematology is a subspecialty of internal medicine, a three-year residency in general internal medicine or pediatrics followed by a three-year fellowship in hematology or hematology-oncology is required. Fellowships focus on adult hematology, hematology/oncology, pathology, pediatric hematology/oncology, and other areas. (For more information on the specifics of medical school, see "Physicians" and "Osteopathic Physicians.")

Certification or Licensing

The American Board of Internal Medicine offers certification in hematology to those who complete training and licensing requirements. The American Board of Pediatrics offers certification in pediatric hematology-oncology. Contact the boards for more information. Some hematologists also choose to become board certified in oncology since this field is so closely related to hematology.

After graduating from medical school, you need to pass the licensing examination administered through the board of medical examiners in the state where you plan to practice. If you want to be certified in a medical specialty, you need to pass the specialty board examination in your field after completing residency requirements.

Other Requirements

Hematologists should be inquisitive and have an interest in medicine and research, as well as strong academic ability, especially in the sciences. You need the discipline to spend long hours writing lengthy grant proposals and researching articles. You also need the ability to be a team player and have patience to conduct lengthy research projects. If you work directly with patients and their families, you should feel comfortable dealing with seriously ill people.

EXPLORING

One good way to learn more about health care careers is to volunteer at a local hospital, clinic, or nursing home. This will allow you to see what it's like to work around other health care professionals and patients and possibly determine exactly where your interests lie. As in any career, reading as much as possible about the profession (such as *Blood* or *The Hematologist*, which are published by the American Society of Hematology, http://www.hematologylibrary.org), talking with a high school counselor, and interviewing those working in the field are other important ways to explore your interest. The society also offers profiles of notable hematologists at http://www.hematology.org/Publications/Legends.

EMPLOYERS

Hematologists are employed at medical centers, university medical schools, private research institutes, and blood banks. Hematologists who are physicians have a wider range of employment opportunities than scientists since they also have the option of clinical practice in addition to, or instead of, research.

STARTING OUT

Hematologists find out about job openings in their field through personal contacts and professional journals. Sometimes a postdoctoral fellowship turns into a permanent job. The competition for research positions at prestigious institutions is keen; there can be hundreds of applicants for one job.

The ability to attract grant money for your lab and all or part of your salary plays a major role in a hematologist's employability. Occasionally, it is even necessary to raise your own funding for a postdoctoral position.

ADVANCEMENT

Hematologists advance by developing and carrying out research that is recognized as significant by their professional peers and that has the ability to draw grant money from the federal government and private foundations. Some hematologists move into administrative positions and become directors of major research projects.

Those in academic positions advance by moving from assistant professor to associate professor to full professor. In this field, the most important criteria for academic promotion are research achievements. Hematologists (or hematologist-oncologists) who are involved in clinical work advance in their profession as more patients are referred to them for specialized treatment.

EARNINGS

First-year medical interns earned $47,458 in 2009, according to the Association of American Medical Colleges. Salaries for hematologists in their first year of practice ranged from $120,000 to $215,000, according to Physicians Search, a physician recruitment agency. Those in practice for three years or longer reported earnings of $155,475 to $473,000 with median annual earnings of $269,298. The mean annual earnings for all physicians who specialize in internal medicine were $183,990 in 2009, according to the U.S. Department of Labor. Physicians in clinical work tend to earn much more than hematologists who concentrate on research. The pay for research scientists is sometimes based on available grant or research funds.

Salaried hematologists usually earn fringe benefits such as health and dental insurance, paid vacations, and the opportunity to participate in retirement plans. Self-employed hematologists must provide their own benefits.

WORK ENVIRONMENT

Hematologists often work in research laboratories as independent researchers and as part of a team. These laboratories can be part of a university, hospital, or government research facility. They may also be part of a teaching staff at a university or medical college. Hematologists who are physicians work in clinics, as part of a group practice, or as a member of a hospital or research team.

OUTLOOK

The U.S. Department of Labor projects that employment for all physicians will grow much faster than the average for all careers through 2018. The job outlook for hematologists is difficult to predict. There are many blood disease questions still to be solved, but the future of research depends on the availability of funding. Another factor that makes the future of this field unpredictable is the fact that other subspecialties are taking over some of the areas previously handled by hematologists. For instance, the relationship between hematology and oncology is growing closer, which could result in hematology eventually being absorbed into oncology. Another example is that coagulation (blood clotting) problems are being taken over by cardiology and neurology because of the role of clotting in heart disease and strokes.

FOR MORE INFORMATION

For information about certification, contact
American Board of Internal Medicine
510 Walnut Street, Suite 1700
Philadelphia, PA 19106-3699
Tel: 800-441-2246
http://www.abim.org

For information about certification, contact
American Board of Pediatrics
111 Silver Cedar Court
Chapel Hill, NC 27514-1692
Tel: 919-929-0461
E-mail: abpeds@abpeds.org
https://www.abp.org

For information about educational training and careers in hematology, contact
American Society of Hematology
2021 L Street, NW, Suite 900
Washington, DC 20036-4929
Tel: 202-776-0544
http://www.hematology.org

Holistic Physicians

QUICK FACTS

School Subjects
Biology
Chemistry
Health

Personal Skills
Helping/teaching
Technical/scientific

Work Environment
Primarily indoors
Primarily multiple locations

Minimum Education Level
Medical degree

Salary Range
$82,360 to $183,990 to
$204,470+

Certification or Licensing
Required for certain
positions (certification)
Required by all states
(licensing)

Outlook
Much faster than the average

DOT
070

GOE
14.02.01

NOC
3112

O*NET-SOC
29-1062.00, 29-1063.00,
29-1064.00, 29-1065.00

OVERVIEW

Holistic physicians are licensed medical doctors who embrace the philosophy of treating the patient as a whole person. Their goal is to help the individual achieve maximum well-being in mind, body, and spirit. Holistic medicine emphasizes a cooperative relationship between physician and patient and focuses on educating patients in taking responsibility for their lives and their health. Holistic physicians use many approaches to diagnosis and treatment, including many other alternative approaches, such as acupuncture, meditation, nutritional counseling, and lifestyle changes. They also use drugs and surgery when a less invasive treatment cannot be found. Holistic physicians are part of the rapidly growing field of complementary and alternative health care practitioners. Most work in private practice or in alternative health clinics.

HISTORY

The modern term *holism* was first used in 1926 by Jan Smuts in *Holism and Evolution*. Smuts championed the idea that living things are much more than just the sum of their parts. He challenged the views of modern medical science, which reduced the individual to a collection of body parts and diseases and denied the complexity of the human experience.

Dr. Evart Loomis is considered by many to be the father of modern holistic medicine. As early as 1940, Dr. Loomis believed that all aspects of an individual had to be considered in order to determine the cause of an

Books to Read

Balch, Phyllis A. *Prescription for Nutritional Healing.* 5th ed. New York: Avery, 2010.

Bratman, Steven. *Collins Alternative Health Guide.* New York: Collins, 2007.

Ernst, Edzard, Max H. Pittler, and Barbara Wider. (eds.) *The Desktop Guide to Complementary and Alternative Medicine: An Evidence-Based Approach.* 2d ed. St. Louis: Mosby, 2006.

Jacobs, Bradly P., and Katherine Gundling. *The American College of Physicians Evidence-Based Guide to Complementary and Alternative Medicine.* Philadelphia: American College of Physicians, 2009.

Lake, James, and David Spiegel. *Complementary and Alternative Treatments in Mental Health Care.* Arlington, Va.: American Psychiatric Publishing, 2006.

Strozier, Anne L., and Joyce E. Carpenter. *Introduction to Alternative and Complementary Therapies.* Binghamton, N.Y.: Haworth Press, 2008.

Tierney, Gillian. *Opportunities in Holistic Health Care Careers.* New York: McGraw-Hill, 2006.

illness. In 1958, he and his wife, Vera, founded Meadowlark, thought to be the first holistic medical retreat center in the United States.

In the late 1950s and early 1960s, the holistic medical movement began to grow as people became increasingly aware that modern medicine did not have all the answers. Many chronic (long-term) conditions did not respond to medical treatment. Some side effects and cures even proved to be worse than the diseases. By the 1970s, *holistic* had become a common term. Currently, the use of holistic principles is increasingly incorporated into individual lifestyles and into the practice of medicine.

THE JOB

In many ways, the primary duties of holistic physicians are much like those of allopathic physicians (conventional doctors). They care for the sick and injured and counsel patients on preventive health care. They take medical histories, examine patients, and diagnose illnesses. Holistic physicians also prescribe and perform diagnostic tests and prescribe medications. They may refer patients to specialists and other health care providers as needed. They use conventional drugs and surgery when less invasive approaches are not appropriate or effective.

An important difference between the practices of allopathic physicians and holistic physicians is the approach to the patient-doctor relationship. Holistic doctors work in partnership with their patients. To establish a partnership relationship, holistic practitioners usually spend more time with their clients than allopathic doctors do. The initial visit for an allopathic practitioner is usually 20 to 30 minutes; holistic doctors usually spend 45 minutes to an hour or more on an initial visit. For conventional physicians, most follow-up visits average seven to 10 minutes, while holistic practitioners take 30 to 45 minutes for the same visits.

During the initial history and physical, holistic physicians ask questions about all aspects of a person's life—not just the immediate symptoms of illness. If holistic practitioners are trained in homeopathy, the interview will be particularly detailed. They want to know about what their patients eat, how they sleep, what their life is like, what their stresses are, what makes them happy or sad, what their goals and beliefs are, and much more. They also ask about health history and overall health. Holistic physicians don't just want to know today's symptoms. They try to find the underlying causes of those symptoms. They listen very carefully, and they do not make personal judgments about their patients' lives. They strive to have an attitude of unconditional positive regard for and acceptance of their patients.

Holistic physicians believe that maintaining health is the best approach to eliminating illness. They discuss their patients' lifestyles, and suggest ways to improve their health and life. Nutrition and exercise are often important components of a wellness program.

Holistic doctors use healing modalities that consider the whole person and support the body's natural healing capabilities. They use a variety of approaches to diagnosis and treatment. For chronic (long-term) problems, they frequently recommend natural methods of treatment that have been shown to be more effective than conventional approaches. They are usually trained in several alternative health modalities themselves, but they may refer patients to a specialist if necessary.

Like other physicians, holistic practitioners prescribe conventional drugs, laboratory tests, or surgery when necessary. They discuss the drugs, tests, or other procedures with their patients in advance. They answer questions and help patients understand their options. Holistic physicians give patients choices and involve them in decisions about their healing program.

In addition to their regular duties as health care providers, holistic physicians must complete a large amount of paperwork. Whether they work in clinics or in private practice, they keep accurate patient records. More and more insurance companies are covering complementary and alternative services that are performed by licensed physicians. Holistic practitioners must frequently submit records to insurance companies in order to be paid for their services.

Those who work in private practice must also supervise the operations of their practices. This can involve interviewing, hiring, and training. Physicians in private practice may spend a large percentage of their time on business matters.

REQUIREMENTS

High School

To become a holistic physician, you will have to study for 11 to 18 years after high school. Preparing for this profession is extremely demanding. Because you'll be entering a premed program in college, you'll want to take as many science classes as you can. Biology, chemistry, and physics will prepare you for college medical courses.

Holistic physicians need excellent communication abilities in order to build successful partnership relationships with their patients. Psychology, English, speech, foreign language, and debate classes can help sharpen your communication skills. Business, mathematics, and computer courses can help you gain the skills you need to be a successful businessperson.

Postsecondary Training

To become a holistic physician, you must first become a conventional physician. In order to do this, you must complete a bachelor's degree and medical school. (For more information on the specifics of medical school, see the articles "Physicians" and "Osteopathic Physicians.")

At the present time, training for competency in holistic or alternative medicine is not a part of regular medical training. At the insistence of many students, nearly a third of all conventional medical schools now include courses in complementary and alternative therapies, but they are still relatively few in number. As interest in complementary and alternative approaches grows, the number of courses available in medical schools will undoubtedly increase. Most holistic physicians train themselves in complementary and alternative modalities through special postgraduate work and continuing education. A few graduate schools now offer specialized programs in complementary and alternative health care approaches and a very few residencies are available.

Certification or Licensing

The American Holistic Medical Association established the American Board of Integrative Holistic Medicine (ABHM) in 1996. The ABHM has developed a core curriculum on which it bases its board certification examination for holistic physicians. A certificate indicates that an individual has met the voluntary education and testing requirements of the organization. See the association's Web site (http://www.holisticboard.org) for more information. The American Association of Integrative Medicine also offers certification to holistic physicians.

All 50 states, the District of Columbia, and the U.S. territories license physicians. To obtain a license, you must graduate from an accredited medical school. You must also pass a licensing exam and complete one to seven years of graduate medical education.

Other Requirements

To be a holistic physician, the whole-person approach to healing must be an integral part of your belief system and your life. You must have a fundamental respect for the dignity of humankind and a strong desire to help others.

Excellent listening, communication, and observational skills are essential. You also need the ability to make quick and good critical judgments and decisions in emergencies.

Practicing holistic medicine requires an open mind and a commitment to lifelong learning. Holistic physicians must be highly self-motivated and have the stamina to survive long hours and pressures of education and practice. You need to have the courage of your convictions and enjoy trail blazing. Even though complementary and alternative health care approaches have become more respected within the medical community in recent years, many physicians still do not accept them. Idealism and high ethical standards are essential. Most holistic physicians also need excellent business skills to run their own practices.

EXPLORING

Since the study of medicine involves such a long, expensive educational process, it is a good idea to explore the field carefully in advance to decide whether a career as a holistic physician is for you. Join science clubs and design projects relating to medicine and health care.

Visit your local health food stores and explore the nutrition and homeopathic sections. Talk with the staff. You may find some very knowledgeable, helpful people. Pick up any alternative newspapers and magazines they have. Volunteer at a hospital or nursing home to see how you feel about working with people who are sick or injured.

Contact the professional associations listed at the end of this article for information. Some offer student membership. Some associations offer Web sites with discussion groups; others have searchable databases. You can ask questions and receive answers from some very prominent people in the field of complementary and alternative health care.

Association Web sites also may have searchable databases of holistic physicians. Find one in your area and make an appointment for a physical exam. Experience how the practitioner works and consider whether you would like to practice medicine this way. Ask the physician about the field. Perhaps that person would be willing to hire you for a summer or part-time position or become your mentor.

EMPLOYERS

The major employers of holistic physicians are physicians who have large practices, group practices, or alternative health clinics. An increasing number of physicians become partners or salaried employees of group practices. Working with a medical group spreads out the cost of medical equipment and other business expenses. In response to public interest and use of alternative approaches, a number of hospitals are opening complementary and alternative health care centers.

Some holistic physicians practice privately or with a partner. More holistic physicians are currently practicing on the East Coast and the West Coast in areas where complementary and alternative health care is already more accepted. However, the demand for holistic physicians is growing in all areas of the country.

STARTING OUT

The medical school you attend will have listings for job openings for physicians. If you have established a particular rapport with a staff member, that person might be able to help you. Professional journals, daily newspapers, and the Internet also have listings.

Networking is one of the best ways to find employment. Join professional organizations, attend meetings, and get to know people in the field. Networking with others in your field gives you a better chance of getting to know physicians who share some of your philosophies about holistic health.

Working in the practice or clinic of another physician who shares your beliefs about the practice of medicine is one of the best ways to get started as a holistic physician. It is hard to learn in isolation. When you interview potential employers, learn about their approaches to medicine. Be sure the setting will help you apply the skills you have learned without compromising what you believe about good health care.

A few holistic physicians go into private practice right away. Some set up a new practice, while others purchase an established practice from a physician who is retiring or moving.

ADVANCEMENT

Holistic physicians can advance in a variety of ways. One who starts out as a salaried employee in a large practice or clinic may eventually become a partner. Holistic practitioners also advance by building their clientele and setting up their own practices or group practices. They sometimes buy the practices of retiring practitioners to add to their own.

Another avenue for advancement is specialization. Holistic practitioners may specialize in traditional medical specialties, such as pediatrics or obstetrics and gynecology, or they may choose to specialize in an area of complementary and alternative medicine, such as acupuncture or homeopathy.

For holistic physicians, continuing education is an important part of advancement. Holistic health care requires even more continual learning than conventional medicine. You will want to keep up on developments in the complementary and alternative modalities that interest you most, such as homeopathy, herbal therapy, Oriental medicine, or nutrition. And, of course, you will have to keep current on changes in conventional medicine.

Teaching, writing, and public speaking are yet other directions for professional improvement. A few holistic physicians become executives with state or national organizations, such as the American Holistic Health Association.

EARNINGS

Holistic physicians generally earn about as much as allopathic physicians who work in the same settings. According to the Association of American Medical Colleges, the average first-year resident received a stipend of about $47,458 a year in 2009, depending on the type of residency, the size of the hospital, and the geographic area. Fifth-year residents earned about $55,570 a year. According to Physicians

Search, a physician recruitment agency, average starting salaries for family practitioners range from $90,000 to $150,000. According to the U.S. Department of Labor, in 2009, general and family practitioners earned salaries that ranged from $82,360 to $193,250. General internists earned average salaries of $183,990. Physicians who work in specialties have the highest earnings. For example, obstetricians and gynecologists have average annual salaries of approximately $204,470.

Of course, earnings vary according to experience, skill, hours worked, geographic region, and many other factors. Some holistic practitioners may earn less because they spend more time with their patients, so they can see fewer in a day. Some make up the difference by charging more per visit.

Benefits vary according to the position of the physician. Those who work for large practices, clinics, or hospitals may receive benefit packages that include sick pay, vacation time, insurance, and other benefits. Those who are partners in a practice or are self-employed must provide their own benefits.

WORK ENVIRONMENT

Holistic physicians work in particularly clean, quiet, comfortable surroundings. In keeping with their emphasis on whole-person relationships, many believe making their offices or clinics comfortable and pleasant is of particular importance. They may use air filtration systems and aromatherapy and choose ergonomically appropriate furniture and work stations.

Most group practices and solo practitioners have an office suite. The suite generally has a reception area. In clinics, several professionals may share this area. Most holistic physicians have a secretary or office staff. The suite also contains examining rooms and treatment rooms. In a clinic where several professionals work, there are usually separate offices for the individual professionals.

Holistic physicians who work in large practices or clinics need to work well in a group environment. They may work under supervision or in a team with other professionals. Those who work alone need a lot of self-discipline and must be highly motivated.

Most holistic physicians work four to five days a week. Some work 40 hours a week, although others put in longer hours. Larger practices and clinics may determine the hours of work, but holistic physicians in private practice can set their own. Evening and weekend hours may be scheduled to accommodate patients' needs. Physicians frequently travel between office and hospital to care for their patients.

OUTLOOK

The *Occupational Outlook Handbook (OOH)* predicts that employment for physicians will grow much faster than the average for all occupations through 2018. Demand for holistic physicians is expected to keep pace with or exceed the demand for conventional physicians due to the recent rapid growth in interest in complementary and alternative health care approaches.

Rising health care costs have caused the government to reexamine the health care system. As efforts to control health care costs increase, the general public, the government, and the insurance industry will turn more and more to physicians who provide cost-effective, quality health care services.

Employment opportunities are expected to be best for primary care physicians, including general and family practitioners, general internists, and general pediatricians. Preventive care specialists and geriatric specialists will be in demand; these are areas in which holistic physicians excel.

The *OOH* predicts that in the future, physicians may be more likely to work fewer hours, retire earlier, earn less, or practice in rural and lower income areas. In addition, with the rising costs of health care, physicians will be more likely to take salaried jobs in group medical practices, clinics, and integrated health care systems instead of opening their own practices.

FOR MORE INFORMATION

For information about integrative medicine and certification, contact
American Association of Integrative Medicine
2750 East Sunshine
Springfield, MO 65804-2047
Tel: 417-881-9995
http://www.aaimedicine.com

For information about naturopathic medicine, contact
American Association of Naturopathic Physicians
4435 Wisconsin Avenue, NW, Suite 403
Washington, DC 20016-1851
Tel: 202-237-8150
http://www.naturopathic.org

For information on board certification for holistic medicine, contact
American Board of Integrative Holistic Medicine
5313 Colorado Street
Duluth, MN 55804-1615

Tel: 218-525-5651
E-mail: nsudak@holisticboard.org
http://www.holisticboard.org

For information on complementary, alternative, and integrative medicine, contact
American College for Advancement in Medicine
8001 Irvine Center Drive, Suite 825
Irvine, CA 92618-2967
Tel: 800-532-3688
http://www.acamnet.org

For information on holistic health, contact
American Holistic Health Association
PO Box 17400
Anaheim, CA 92817-7400
Tel: 714-779-6152
E-mail: mail@ahha.org
http://ahha.org

For principles of holistic medical practice, a searchable database of members, and to learn more about the AHMA Newsletter, *contact*
American Holistic Medical Association (AHMA)
23366 Commerce Park, Suite 101B
Beachwood, OH 44122-5801
Tel: 216-292-6644
E-mail: info@holisticmedicine.org
http://www.holisticmedicine.org

Homeopaths

QUICK FACTS

School Subjects
Biology
Chemistry
English

Personal Skills
Helping/teaching
Technical/scientific

Work Environment
Primarily indoors
Primarily one location

Minimum Education Level
Some postsecondary training

Salary Range
$53,539 to $71,320 to
$99,098+

Certification or Licensing
Voluntary (certification)
Required by certain states
(licensing)

Outlook
Faster than the average

DOT
N/A

GOE
N/A

NOC
3232

O*NET-SOC
N/A

OVERVIEW

Samuel Hahnemann, the founder of homeopathy, said, "The highest ideal of cure is the speedy, gentle, and enduring restoration of health by the most trustworthy and least harmful way." *Homeopaths* are health care professionals who practice a complete system of natural medicine called homeopathy. Homeopathic care generally costs less than conventional medical care, and homeopathic medicine is safe, effective, and natural. Homeopathy is used to maintain good health and to treat acute as well as chronic ailments. It has proven to be effective in many instances where conventional medicines have been unsuccessful. Some of its remedies are simple enough to be used by people who are not medically trained.

Homeopathy is part of the rapidly growing field of alternative/complementary health care. Unlike conventional medicine, it does not treat just the symptoms of a disease. Instead, it seeks the underlying cause of the illness. It seeks to stimulate the patient's natural defenses and the immune system so the body can heal itself. Homeopaths believe that being healthy means being balanced mentally, emotionally, and physically. In this sense, homeopathy is truly a holistic medical model.

HISTORY

Samuel Hahnemann, a renowned German physician, founded homeopathy in 1796. Medical practices in the 1700s and 1800s often caused more harm than good. Physicians routinely used bloodletting, purging, and large doses of toxic medicines as part of their treatments. Dr. Hahnemann wanted to find a more humane approach. Through years of careful observation, experimentation, and documentation, he developed the system of medicine that he named homeopathy. Homeopathy grew because it was systematic, effective, and comparatively inexpensive. Precisely because of its benefits, the new system threatened the medical establishment. Dr. Hahnemann was persecuted and even arrested. However, he was determined and courageous, and he continued his work throughout his life. His system of medicine spread throughout the world.

Several doctors who had studied homeopathy in Europe immigrated to the United States around 1825. They introduced homeopathy to other physicians, and its popularity grew rapidly. By the mid-1800s, several medical colleges in the United States taught homeopathy. In 1844, homeopaths established the first national medical society in America, the American Institute of Homeopathy. The practice of homeopathy continued to thrive until the early 1900s. At the turn of the century, the United States had 22 homeopathic medical colleges, and one-fifth of the country's medical doctors used homeopathy.

However, like Hahnemann in Europe, the homeopaths in the United States seemed to pose a threat to the conventional medical and pharmaceutical establishments. For a variety of reasons— attacks by the medical establishment, growth in popularity of a more "mechanical" model of medicine, and discord among homeopaths themselves—the practice of homeopathy in the United States declined. By the late 1940s, there were no homeopathy courses taught in this country.

Homeopaths in other countries also experienced opposition. However, homeopathy flourished wherever people were allowed to practice it with relative freedom. Today, more than 500 million people worldwide receive homeopathic treatment. Homeopathy is popular in England, France, Germany, the Netherlands, India, Pakistan, Sri Lanka, Brazil, and many other countries. Because homeopathic treatments and drugs are natural and relatively inexpensive, even countries with limited resources can take advantage of them. In this country, there has been a tremendous increase in interest in homeopathy since the 1970s. Statistics show that Americans are turning to this form of treatment in dramatic numbers. As complementary/alternative health care is growing, so is the field of homeopathy.

THE JOB

Homeopaths help people improve their lives and get well. They look at illness differently than conventional doctors do. They view the symptoms of an illness as the body's attempts to heal itself. For example, they see a cough as the body's efforts to rid itself of something that is foreign to the system. Instead of trying to suppress the symptoms, homeopaths search for the underlying cause of the problem. They try to discover the more fundamental reason for the illness. Why was the body susceptible to a cough in the first place?

To homeopaths, people are healthy when their lives are balanced mentally, emotionally, and physically. If any aspect of the patient's life is out of balance, it could lead to illness. A symptom, such as a cough, is just the top layer of a problem, and homeopaths work to peel away all the layers and get to the root of the problem. The goal of homeopathic medicine is not just to cure the ailment, but rather to return the individual to optimum health.

To discover the reasons for an illness, homeopaths begin with a very detailed individual interview. The first interview usually takes at least an hour and may last up to two hours. Homeopathic treatment is based entirely on the individual. Homeopaths believe that every person is unique and that individuals experience the same illness differently. Although two people may complain of a cold, each of them will have unique symptoms and be affected in different ways. The homeopathic practitioner asks questions about every aspect of the individual's life—health symptoms, eating habits, sleeping patterns, reactions to heat and chill, and so on. In order to process all of this information, homeopaths must have good communication and analytical skills and be very attentive to detail. Choosing the right cure depends on understanding every aspect of the individual's situation, not just the illness.

To help guide their research, homeopaths classify people into categories called constitutional types. They determine an individual's constitutional type according to temperament, physical appearance, emotional history, previous ailments, preferences about food, reactions to the weather, and many other traits. Then they search for a constitutional medicine, one that produces symptoms that are most similar to the individual's symptoms.

Homeopathy is based upon the principle that "like cures like," also called the Law of Similars. Dr. Hahnemann observed that a substance that produces the symptoms of an illness when given in a large dose could cure the illness if it were given in a minute dose. The theory is that the small dose stimulates the body's natural healing power to fight off the illness. Hippocrates, the Greek physician who is considered to be the father of medicine, first recognized this principle in 4 B.C. The Law of Similars is also the theory behind some conventional medicines, such as vaccinations and allergy shots.

After determining the individual's constitutional type, homeopaths seek out the substance that is capable of producing the same symptoms that the individual is experiencing. They can spend much of their day at the office studying their notes and researching. They search through books called repertories or use computers and the Internet to find the right constitutional medicine.

Homeopaths use very small doses of natural medicines to stimulate the body to heal itself. The Law of the Infinitesimal Dose is another important principle of homeopathic medicine. It states that the more dilute a remedy is, the more powerful it is. Although this seems paradoxical, years of clinical study have shown the small doses to be effective.

Homeopathic medicines are natural, safe, and effective. They are specially prepared from plant, animal, or mineral extracts. The raw material is dissolved in a mixture of alcohol and water. Then it is diluted several times and shaken vigorously. The Food and Drug Administration (FDA) recognizes homeopathic remedies as official drugs. It regulates their production, labeling, and distribution just as it does conventional medicines. Homeopathic remedies are collected in an official compendium, the *Homeopathic Pharmacopocia of the United States*, which was first published in 1894.

After homeopaths choose a remedy, they instruct the individual in its use. This may happen at the end of the initial interview if the person's symptoms point to an obvious cure. Many times, however, homeopaths must spend a long time searching for the remedy that matches the essence of the person's symptoms. When that is the case, they may not give the individual a remedy at the first session. Finding the exact constitutional medicine requires patience, experience, problem-solving ability, and intuition.

The course of treatment depends on the individual's circumstances, symptoms, and prognosis. After a prescribed period of time, the individual generally returns for a follow-up visit. This visit typically lasts from 15 to 45 minutes. During this time, homeopaths look for signs of improvement and sometimes choose a different remedy if the desired result has not been obtained. Usually only one remedy is given at a time because the goal is to stimulate the body's natural defenses with a minimal amount of medicine. Homeopaths tend to discourage frequent visits unless they are medically necessary. The time between visits is usually from one to six months.

Most homeopaths work in private practice, so they must know how to handle paperwork and run a business. Many are health

contact the national homeopathic associations listed at the end of this article for information about programs, requirements, and scholarship funds.

Certification or Licensing

Certification indicates that a homeopath has met the standards of education and knowledge set by a particular professional association. The Council for Homeopathic Certification offers the certified in classical homeopathy credential to those who pass written and oral examinations. Contact the council for more information about certification.

An individual can be a certified homeopath but still not be licensed to practice medicine. Licensing is a requirement established by government. Homeopaths who are licensed health care practitioners in other fields, such as chiropractors, physicians, naturopathic physicians, nurses, and nurse practitioners, must maintain the appropriate licenses for their specific fields.

Both certification and licensing requirements for homeopaths vary according to state. Some states do not consider homeopathy to be the practice of medicine, so they do not regulate its practice. Other states require homeopaths to be licensed in some other form of health care. Arizona, Connecticut, and Nevada offer homeopathic medical licenses. Check with the office of the attorney general in your state to be sure you know its certification and licensing requirements. Although some homeopaths currently practice without a medical license, professionals in the field agree that the trend is toward certification and licensing. If you are interested in a career in homeopathy, it is recommended that you acquire a license in some related field of medicine.

Other Requirements

To be a successful homeopath, you need to enjoy helping and working with people. On the other hand, you must also be self-motivated and enjoy researching and working alone. You need to be inquisitive, detail oriented, independent, and self-reliant. It helps to enjoy solving mysteries and puzzles.

In addition, you must know your own mind and have the courage of your convictions. Because homeopathy is reemerging as an important form of complementary and alternative health care in this country, homeopaths need to have strong convictions and be able to take criticism. They may have to defend their work or try to educate others who know little about homeopathy. It helps for a homeopath to be a bit of a crusader.

EXPLORING

There are many ways for you to learn about homeopathy right now. Ask your librarian for homeopathic journals, newsletters (such as *Homeopathy Today*, http://nationalcenterforhomeopathy.org/media/homeopathy_today), and books. Visit your local health food stores and explore the homeopathic section. Talk with the staff. You may find some very knowledgeable, helpful people. Pick up any alternative newspapers and magazines they have. Ask if there are homeopathic practitioners or pharmacists in the area. If there are, visit them, and talk to them about their work. There are still relatively few homeopaths in this country, but they are generally enthusiastic supporters of others who are interested in the career. Surf the Internet. There is a wealth of information online, and there are alternative medicine/holistic health forums where you can discuss homeopathic medicine with people in the field. If possible, make an appointment with a homeopath so you can experience this approach to health care for yourself.

The National Center for Homeopathy has information on training sessions and seminars located throughout the country where beginners can study. Students can study a variety of topics and live and learn with others interested in the field, from beginners to experts.

EMPLOYERS

Most homeopaths practice on their own or with a partner. Working with a partner makes practicing easier because the costs of running an office are shared. Other tasks, such as bookkeeping and record keeping can also be shared. Alternative health clinics and some other health care professionals may hire homeopaths. Hospitals and other health care agencies generally do not hire homeopaths, but they may as the complementary/alternative health care movement grows.

It is easier to practice homeopathy in some areas of the United States, such as on the West Coast and in larger cities, but there are practicing homeopaths throughout the country.

STARTING OUT

Since homeopaths come from so many different backgrounds, ways to get started vary, too. Licensed professionals generally begin practicing the discipline in which they are licensed. Some build their homeopathic practice along with the other practice. Others just begin a homeopathic practice. Unlicensed homeopaths may work with licensed individuals. In these cases, the licensed professional is generally legally responsible for the work of the unlicensed homeopath. Some unlicensed individuals have been known to offer their services for free at the beginning, just to gain experience.

Homeopathy is a growing field, but it is still a relatively small community of professionals. Once you get to know others in the field, you may be able to find a mentor who will help you learn how to get started. Networking with others in the field can be an extremely valuable way to learn and grow.

ADVANCEMENT

Advancement comes with building a solid reputation. Homeopaths whose practices grow may eventually need to look for partners in order to take care of more patients. Many homeopaths are active promoters of the discipline. They write articles for journals or magazines or present information on homeopathy in public forums, such as on radio and television.

Others pursue research into homeopathic treatments and present their findings to colleagues at conventions or publish their work in the homeopathic journals. A few may work with the homeopathic pharmaceutical companies.

EARNINGS

Since many homeopaths are in solo practice, incomes vary widely according to the number of hours worked and the rates charged. Statistics on earnings in the field are not yet available, but professionals tend to agree that homeopathic physicians charge between $100 and $300 for an initial visit of 60 to 90 minutes and $50 to $100 for a follow-up visit of 15 to 45 minutes. Unlicensed homeopaths charge between $50 and $250 for the same initial visit and $30 to $80 for a follow-up. They may take several years to build a practice, and their rates will usually remain on the lower end of the scale. Fees tend to increase the longer the individual has been practicing. The State University Web site (http://careers.stateuniversity.com/pages/7829/Homeopath.html) reports salaries for homeopaths range from $53,539 to $99,098, with median earnings of $71,320.

According to Dana Ullman, nationally known expert on homeopathy, licensed professionals earn about the average for their professions or a little less. For example, homeopathic physicians earn $90,000 to $175,000 a year. They have good incomes, but generally not as high as the average medical doctor. (Mean earnings of general practitioners in 2009 were $168,550, according to the

U.S. Department of Labor.) Other licensed professionals, such as homeopathic nurses, might earn $60,000 to $100,000. Unlicensed homeopaths usually earn less, perhaps beginning around $30,000. As with all self-employed individuals, income is directly related to number of hours worked and fees charged.

Since most homeopaths are solo practitioners, they must supply their own benefits, such as vacations, insurance, and retirement funds. In addition, licensed professionals must maintain their licenses and pay for their own malpractice insurance.

WORK ENVIRONMENT

Homeopaths work indoors, usually in their own offices, and sometimes even in their homes. As a result, they have the surroundings of their choice. Since they meet with patients and also spend time in research, they frequently have quiet, pleasant offices. Most work on their own with little, if any, supervision, so it is important to be self-motivated. Many homeopaths also have the ability to determine the number of hours and days they work per week. They may set schedules that make it easy for their patients to make appointments.

OUTLOOK

The field of homeopathy is growing rapidly along with the national interest in alternative health care. Homeopathy can be combined with a variety of health care professions. Many practitioners include it among other healing approaches they use. However, many homeopaths believe that it is best to specialize in homeopathy. The amount of experience and the complexity of the knowledge required to become a good practitioner make homeopathy a lifelong education.

The World Health Organization (WHO), the medical branch of the United Nations, cited homeopathy as one of the systems of traditional medicine that should be integrated worldwide with conventional medicine in order to provide adequate global health care in the next century. The field of homeopathy is growing faster than the average.

FOR MORE INFORMATION

This national organization certifies practitioners of classical homeopathy.

Council for Homeopathic Certification
PMB 187
16915 SE 272nd Street, Suite 100

Covington, WA 98042-7347
Tel: 866-242-3399
http://www.homeopathicdirectory.com

For comprehensive Internet information on complementary and alternative health care in general and homeopathy in particular as well as extensive links, visit
HealthWorld Online
http://www.healthy.net

Homeopathic Educational Services
http://www.homeopathic.com

Homeopathy Home
http://www.homeopathyhome.com

This professional association provides education and training for homeopathic professionals and for interested consumers who want to learn homeopathy for their own use.
National Center for Homeopathy
101 South Whiting Street, Suite 16
Alexandria, VA 22304-3416
Tel: 703-548-7790
E-mail: info@nationalcenterforhomeopathy.org
http://homeopathic.org

For information on education and homeopathic research, contact
North American Society of Homeopaths
PO Box 450039
Sunrise, FL 33345-0039
Tel: 206-720-7000
E-mail: NashInfo@homeopathy.org
http://www.homeopathy.org

Neurologists

OVERVIEW

Neurologists are physician specialists who diagnose and treat patients with diseases and disorders affecting such areas as the brain, spinal cord, peripheral nerves, muscles, and autonomic nervous system.

HISTORY

The development of modern neurology began in the 18th and 19th centuries. Studies were performed on animals in order to understand how the human brain functioned. Although these early studies produced some useful information, major research in the field of neurology did not begin until the end of the 19th century. Aphasia, epilepsy, and motor problems were targeted and researched. Techniques for brain mapping were also introduced in an effort to determine the locations of functional areas.

In 1924, Hans Berger invented the electroencephalograph, which records the electrical activity in the brain. This achievement led to greater capabilities in diagnosis, treatment, and rehabilitation. During the late 20th century, neurology was further advanced by computerized axial tomography (CAT scans), nuclear magnetic resonance, and neurosurgery.

By the 21st century, continued research led to better drug therapies and a clearer understanding of brain function. Results of this research have given neurologists such resources as new surgical techniques and treatments, including implanted "pacemakers" for certain types of epilepsy; they have also increased their understanding of the causes of neuropathic pain, provided new drug treatments for migraines, and resulted in the discovery

QUICK FACTS

School Subjects
Biology
Health

Personal Skills
Helping/teaching
Technical/scientific

Work Environment
Primarily indoors
Primarily multiple locations

Minimum Education Level
Medical degree

Salary Range
$174,562 to $205,757 to $244,583+

Certification or Licensing
Required for certain positions (certification)
Required by all states (licensing)

Outlook
Much faster than the average

DOT
070

GOE
14.02.01

NOC
3112

O*NET-SOC
29-1067.00, 29-1069.04

of genetic links for certain conditions. As the field of neurology continues to grow, treatments and—in some cases—cures are being found for diseases that previously had not even been identified with a name.

THE JOB

A neurologist evaluates, diagnoses, and treats patients with diseases and disorders impairing the function of the brain, spinal cord, peripheral nerves, muscles, and autonomic nervous system, as well as the supporting structures and vascular supply to these areas. A neurologist conducts and evaluates specific tests relating to the analysis of the central or peripheral nervous system.

In addition to treating such neurological disorders as epilepsy, neuritis, brain and spinal cord tumors, multiple sclerosis, Parkinson's disease, and stroke, neurologists treat muscle disorders and pain, especially headache. Illnesses, injuries, or diseases that can adversely affect the nervous system, such as diabetes, hypertension, and cancers, are also treated by neurologists.

Neurologists see patients in two capacities—as a consulting physician or as the patient's principal physician. A neurologist works as a consulting physician when asked by a patient's primary care physician to consult on a case. For example, when a patient has a stroke or shows signs of mental confusion, that patient's primary care doctor may ask a neurologist to consult on the case so that they can determine exactly what is wrong with the patient. In this circumstance, as a consulting physician, the neurologist conducts a neurological examination and evaluates the patient's mental, emotional, and behavioral problems to assess whether these conditions are treatable. To do the exam, the neurologist may interview the patient, give vision, balance, and strength tests, and order a magnetic resonance imaging scan (MRI) of the person's brain. After the neurologist has gathered information from a variety of sources, he or she will discuss the findings with the primary care doctor and make a diagnosis. Treatment plans are then made.

A neurologist is often the principal physician for people with such illnesses as Parkinson's disease, epilepsy, or multiple sclerosis. Because these are chronic and sometimes progressive conditions, the neurologist monitors the development of the illness and works to treat the patient's symptoms, which may include muscle spasms, seizures, or loss of coordination. The neurologist may prescribe medications (such as an anticonvulsant), physical therapy (to maintain strength or coordination), or new tests (such as a CAT scan). Depending on the patient's condition, the neurologist may see the patient anywhere from every few months to once a year.

The neurologist also works with psychiatrists, psychologists, and other mental health professionals as necessary, because a patient's social condition and emotional issues are closely tied to neurological health. Patients with dementia, for example, often also suffer from depression. When a neurologist notices that a patient being treated seems withdrawn and unusually down, the neurologist may call in a psychiatrist to determine if anything can be done to help with the patient's emotional needs.

REQUIREMENTS

High School

Neurologists first earn an M.D. degree and become licensed to practice medicine. If you are interested in pursuing a medical degree, a high school education emphasizing college preparatory classes is a must. Science courses, such as biology, chemistry, and physics, are necessary, as are math courses. These classes will not only provide you with an introduction to basic science and math concepts but also allow you to determine your own aptitude in these areas. Since college will be your next educational step, it is also important to take English courses to develop your research and writing skills. Foreign language and social science classes will also help make you an appealing candidate for college admission as well as prepare you for your future undergraduate and graduate education. Courses in computer science are a must, as well, since the computer is changing the way medicine is communicated and shared by busy medical professionals.

Postsecondary Training

In order to become a neurologist, you must first earn an M.D. or D.O. (see "Physicians" and "Osteopathic Physicians"). Those physicians who choose to specialize in adult neurology must first complete an internship (with a minimum of eight months spent in internal medicine) and a three-year residency in neurology. Both the internship and residency must be accredited by the Accreditation Council for Graduate Medical Education (ACGME). Those wanting to work in child neurology have several training pathways to choose from, including completing two years of a pediatrics residency or one-year residencies in internal medicine and pediatrics. Again, these must be ACGME accredited. In addition, there are a growing number of programs that combine fields and prepare graduates to be eligible for certification in two areas, such as neurology/internal medicine or neurology/psychiatry. The residency programs provide supervised neurology experience in both hospital and ambulatory (outpatient) settings. Educational conferences and research training are also part of a neurology residency. Visit the council's Web site, http://www.acgme.org/adspublic, for a list of accredited programs.

Certification or Licensing

Upon completion of residency training, neurologists may seek certification in neurology or child neurology from the American Board of Psychiatry and Neurology (ABPN). To be eligible for certification, qualified applicants must have an unrestricted state license to practice medicine; have the required years of residency training; and must pass both a written and oral examination as administered by the ABPN.

All physicians must be licensed to practice in the United States. To become licensed, physicians must pass a state exam, which is administered by their state's board of medical examiners.

Other Requirements

Because they treat patients who may have suffered injuries to the head, neurologists need to have a calm and soothing presence with patients who may be experiencing alternating emotions, including confusion and anger. In addition to compassion, neurologists need to be capable of sifting through a lot of data for specific details.

EARNINGS

Individual salaries for neurologists vary depending on such factors as type and size of practice, geographic area, and professional reputation. First-year interns earned $47,458 in 2009, according to the Association of American Medical Colleges. In 2009, salaries for neurologists ranged from less than $174,562 to more than $244,583, with median annual earnings of $205,757, according to a survey by Salary.com. Because of the variety of factors influencing earnings, these figures should only be thought of as a guide.

Neurologists working for hospitals, research institutes, and universities receive typical benefits such as paid vacation time, health insurance, and retirement plans. Those who run their own practices must pay for such benefits themselves.

OUTLOOK

The U.S. Department of Labor (DOL) predicts that employment for physicians in general should grow much faster than the average for all careers through 2018. Although the DOL does not provide an employment prediction for neurologists, it does note, however, that patient demand should create a substantial number of jobs for specialists. The future for neurologists, therefore, should be bright as the need for their expertise increases. One reason for this increased need is the country's growing senior population. Older people are often affected by neurological problems, including a wide variety of dementias. As research continues and treatments become available there should be more resources neurologists can draw on to help patients manage such diseases as Alzheimer's. Additionally, research should provide answers to questions about what causes certain diseases and why and how these diseases progress. When doctors know these answers, they will be able to provide increasingly accurate treatments for such illnesses as amyotrophic lateral sclerosis (Lou Gehrig's disease), multiple sclerosis, and Parkinson's disease. For these reasons, neurologists should experience strong job growth.

FOR MORE INFORMATION

For information on careers in neurology, contact
American Academy of Neurology
1080 Montreal Avenue
St. Paul, MN 55116-2386
Tel: 800-879-1960
http://www.aan.com

For information about neurological surgery, contact
American Association of Neurological Surgeons
5550 Meadowbrook Drive
Rolling Meadows, IL 60008-3845
Tel: 888-566-2267
E-mail: info@aans.org
http://www.aans.org

For information on certification, contact
American Board of Psychiatry and Neurology
2150 East Lake Cook Road, Suite 900
Buffalo Grove, IL 60089-1875
Tel: 847-229-6500
E-mail: questions@abpn.com
http://www.abpn.com

For information about academic neurology, visit the association's Web site.
American Neurological Association
5841 Cedar Lake Road, Suite 204
Minneapolis, MN 55416-5657
Tel: 952-545-6284
E-mail: ana@llmsi.com
http://www.aneuroa.org

Obstetricians/ Gynecologists

QUICK FACTS

School Subjects
Biology
Health

Personal Skills
Helping/teaching
Technical/scientific

Work Environment
Primarily indoors
Primarily multiple locations

Minimum Education Level
Medical degree

Salary Range
$99,520 to $204,470 to
$210,450+

Certification or Licensing
Required for certain
positions (certification)
Required by all states
(licensing)

Outlook
Much faster than the average

DOT
070

GOE
14.02.01

NOC
3112

O*NET-SOC
29-1064.00, 29-1067.00

OVERVIEW

Obstetricians/gynecologists, often abbreviated *OB/GYNs,* are physicians who are trained to provide medical and surgical care for disorders that affect the female reproductive system, to deliver babies, and to provide care for the unborn fetus and the newborn. There are approximately 20,380 physicians who specialize in obstetrics/gynecology in the United States.

HISTORY

Obstetrics and gynecology were recognized medical disciplines in the United States by the middle of the 19th century. However, these two fields developed separately throughout history and differently across cultural boundaries.

Female midwives were the first individuals to perform obstetric work. It was not until the 17th century that European physicians became involved in childbirth. Aristocrats and royalty allowed these physicians to attend the births of their children, and eventually the practice spread to the middle classes.

Gynecology evolved separately from obstetrics but was practiced in Greco-Roman civilization and possibly earlier. Despite their separate early histories, the similar nature of obstetrics and gynecology forced the disciplines to merge. Both fields were advanced by the invention of the forceps used during delivery, anesthesia, and antiseptic methods used during gynecologic

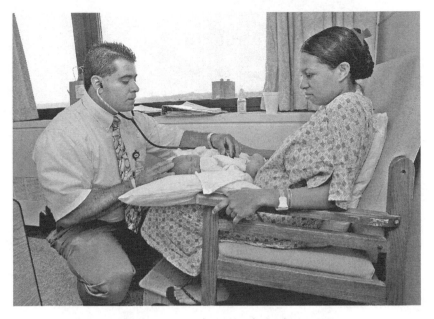

An obstetrician examines a newborn and mother. *(Dick Blume, Syracuse Newspapers/The Image Work)*

surgery and childbirth. The method of cesarean section as an alternative to natural childbirth was also a major advancement in early medical practice.

Fertility, the promotion of healthy births, and prenatal care define the scope of obstetric and gynecologic advances now seen in the 21st century. Hormonal contraceptive pills were introduced in the 1950s and helped to regulate women's fertility, while the development of amniocentesis and ultrasound allowed for more accurate prenatal diagnosis of birth disorders.

THE JOB

The specialty of obstetrics and gynecology can be divided into two parts. Obstetrics focuses on the care and treatment of women before their pregnancy, during the pregnancy, and after the child is born. Gynecology is concerned with the treatment of diseases and disorders of the female reproductive system. Because the areas overlap, the specialties are generally practiced together. Preventive measures and testing make up a large part of an OB/GYN's practice.

Obstetricians/gynecologists provide many different types of health services to women, from prenatal care to Pap tests to screening tests

Did You Know?

During the 1930s, Dr. George Papanicolaou found that cervical cancer could be detected by studying cells from a woman's genital tract. This led to the development of the Pap test, now a routine gynecological procedure used to detect cervical cancer. According to the American Cancer Society, the Pap test, along with regular gynecological checkups, has reduced deaths caused by cervical cancer by 70 percent over the past 40 years. Approximately 55 million Pap tests are performed annually in the United States, according to the National Cancer Institute.

for sexually transmitted diseases to breast exams and birth control. With specialization, the OB/GYN's practice may focus on pregnant patients, cancer patients, or infertile patients.

Disorders that OB/GYNs commonly treat include yeast infections, pelvic pain, endometriosis, infertility, and uterine and ovarian cancer. The doctor prescribes medicines and other therapies and, if necessary, schedules and performs surgery.

When an examination and test indicate that a patient is pregnant, an OB/GYN sets up regular appointments with the patient throughout the pregnancy. These visits make up a crucial part of any woman's prenatal care, helping her learn about her pregnancy, nutrition and diet, and activities that could adversely affect the pregnancy. In addition, the patient is examined to see that the pregnancy is progressing normally. Later in the pregnancy, the frequency of visits increases, and they become important in determining a birthing strategy and any alternate plans. An OB/GYN will deliver the baby and care for the mother and child after the delivery.

REQUIREMENTS

High School

You can prepare for a future in medicine by taking courses in biology, chemistry, physics, algebra, geometry, and trigonometry. Courses in computer science are a must, as well, since the computer is changing the way medicine is communicated and shared by medical professionals. Also important are courses such as English and speech that foster good communication skills, as well as taking a foreign language.

Postsecondary Training

In order to earn an M.D., you must complete four years of medical school (see "Physicians"). Then you must complete a minimum of four years in residency, three of them entirely in obstetrics and gynecology, with a one-year elective. According to the American Board of Obstetrics and Gynecology, residency topics include genetic counseling and prenatal diagnosis, preconceptional health, pregnancy, labor and childbirth, postpartum care, and genetics.

Students can also attend an osteopathic medical program leading to the Doctor of Osteopathic Medicine degree. (See "Osteopathic Physicians" for more information.)

After completing a residency in obstetrics and gynecology, a specialist in obstetrics and gynecology may pursue additional training to subspecialize in critical care medicine, gynecologic oncology, maternal-fetal medicine, or reproductive endocrinology.

Certification or Licensing

Certification by the American Board of Obstetrics and Gynecology (ABOG) is highly recommended. In the last months of your residency, you take the written examination given by the ABOG. Candidates for certification take the final oral examination after two or more years of practice. You must have successfully passed the written portion of the certifying exam before you are eligible to take the oral portion. The ABOG also offers certification in the following subspecialties: maternal-fetal medicine, reproductive endocrinology and infertility, female pelvic medicine and reconstructive surgery, and gynecologic oncology.

New physicians are required to take an examination to be licensed to practice. Every state requires such an examination. It is conducted through the board of medical examiners in each state.

Other Requirements

Communication skills are essential, as most of your time is spent with patients, talking to them and listening to their histories and problems. The intimate nature of both the patient's condition and the examination requires that an OB/GYN be able to put the patient at ease while asking questions of an intimate nature.

EARNINGS

Salaries for obstetricians/gynecologists vary according to the kind of practice (whether he or she works individually or as part of a group practice), the amount of overhead required to maintain the practice, and the geographic location. First-year interns earned $47,458 in

2009, according to the Association of American Medical Colleges. According to the U.S. Department of Labor, OB/GYNs earned mean salaries of $204,470 in 2009. Salaries for OB/GYNs ranged from less than $99,520 to $210,450 or more. Fringe benefits for OB/GYNs typically include health and dental insurance, paid vacations, and retirement plans. Self-employed OB/GYNs must provide their own benefits.

OUTLOOK

According to the *Occupational Outlook Handbook*, the employment of physicians is expected to grow much faster than the average for all occupations through 2018.

Opportunities for OB/GYNs should be even better. The demand for OB/GYNs has not abated. In fact, some experts predict that there will be shortages of these professionals as OB/GYNs continue to leave the field on account of soaring malpractice insurance premiums and smaller Medicaid reimbursements. Opportunities should be especially good for OB/GYNs who are willing to work in rural or other underserved areas.

FOR MORE INFORMATION

For information on certification, contact
American Board of Obstetrics and Gynecology
2915 Vine Street
Dallas, TX 75204-1045
Tel: 214-871-1619
http://www.abog.org

For information on obstetrics and gynecology, contact
American Congress of Obstetricians and Gynecologists
PO Box 96920
Washington, DC 20090-6920
Tel: 202-638-5577
http://www.acog.org

For information on subspecialties in the field, contact
Society for Maternal-Fetal Medicine
409 12th Street, SW
Washington, DC 20024-2125
Tel: 202-863-2476
E-mail: smfm@smfm.org
https://www.smfm.org

Oncologists

OVERVIEW

Oncologists are physicians who study, diagnose, and treat the tumors caused by cancer. When an individual is diagnosed with cancer, an oncologist takes charge of the patient's overall care and treatment through all phases of the disease. There are three primary areas within clinical oncology: medical oncology, surgical oncology, and radiation oncology.

HISTORY

The history of cancer dates back to early Greek and Roman writings, which included descriptions of the disease. It is clear that cancer affects all of the world's populations and has been the subject of intense medical investigations. According to the American Cancer Society, approximately 1.5 million people in the United States are diagnosed with cancer each year. Cancer ranks second only to heart disease as the leading cause of death.

Developments in the late 20th century, such as improvements in cancer treatment and early detection, have advanced the discipline of oncology and led to further studies. In the 1950s, minor success with cytotoxic chemotherapy initiated active research to develop anticancer agents. Although most useful drugs have side effects, oncologists continue to conduct studies to find better treatments. Increased public awareness of the positive effects of a healthy diet and exercise as well as the harmful effects of smoking and excessive drinking has helped lower the risk of developing many types of cancer. Many believe that cancer will someday become a largely preventable—or at least manageable—disease.

THE JOB

An oncologist is a physician who specializes in the study, diagnosis, and treatment of cancerous tumors. Because cancer can affect any organ in the body, and individuals of any age, there are many different kinds of oncologists. For example, *medical oncologists* have studied internal medicine and treat cancer through chemotherapy. *Pediatric oncologists* are pediatricians who specialize in cancers that affect infants and children. *Gynecological oncologists* specialize in cancers that attack the female reproductive organs, including the ovary, cervix, and uterus. *Radiation oncologists* treat tumors through radiation therapy. *Surgical oncologists* are surgeons who specialize in removing cancerous tissue to prevent its growth. There are many other subspecialties within the practice of oncology. In fact, there are almost as many different subspecialties of oncology as there are different kinds of doctors.

A *clinical oncologist* conducts clinical trials in order to identify the most successful strategies for fighting cancer. Clinical trials are studies that are conducted on consenting patients. By comparing the results of two different treatments on two groups of patients with similar symptoms, clinical oncologists are able to determine which methods are more effective in eliminating or retarding the development of cancer.

Because cancer can spread throughout the organs of the body, oncologists often work together in teams to identify the appropriate strategy for helping a patient. Because many patients undergo a combination of chemotherapy, radiation therapy, and surgery to treat cancer, it is extremely important for the physicians to coordinate the treatment process.

Oncologists, like many physicians, divide their time between patient consultations, medical procedures, study, research, publishing, and office or departmental administration. Most oncologists work more than 40 hours per week.

Oncologists may see anywhere from 10 to 30 patients each day. In many of these encounters, they may have to deliver devastating health news regarding a malignancy and help patients make extremely difficult choices. They explain the various treatment options, the toxic side effects associated with each option, and give patients realistic assessments of their chances of recovery. As patients undergo treatment, oncologists also help them cope with the pain and discomfort caused both by the disease and the treatment methods.

REQUIREMENTS

High School

If you are interested in a career as an oncologist, the first step is to take high school college preparatory courses. Science courses, such as biology, chemistry, physics, and anatomy, will help prepare you for college. Math courses, such as algebra, geometry, and trigonometry, are also important. English and speech classes will help you develop your research, writing, and oral communication skills. Computer science courses are essential. Foreign language courses are also recommended.

Postsecondary Training

Your next step in becoming an oncologist is to earn a bachelor's degree at an accredited college or university. Students who plan to go to medical school typically major in a science, such as biology or chemistry. Regardless of the major, course work should emphasize the sciences and include classes such as biology, chemistry, anatomy, and physiology. Other important classes to take include mathematics, such as calculus, English, ethics, and psychology. Volunteering or working at a hospital during your college years is also an excellent way to gain experience working in a medical setting.

After graduating from medical school (see "Physicians" and "Osteopathic Physicians"), you must pass a standard exam given by the National Board of Medical Examiners. You then complete an internship or transition year during which you decide your area of specialization.

Following your medical schooling and internship, you complete a residency in your chosen specialty. For example, someone interested in gynecologic oncology completes a four-year obstetrics and gynecology residency. Someone interested in medical oncology, on the other hand, does a residency in internal medicine. Following the residency, you will complete a fellowship (specialized study) in oncology. A fellowship in gynecologic oncology, for example, can take from two to four years to complete.

Certification or Licensing

Certification is highly recommended. Certification for oncologists is administered by boards in their area of specialty. For example, certification for medical oncologists is administered by the American Board of Internal Medicine (http://www.abim.org). Certification for gynecologic oncologists is administered by the American Board of Obstetrics and Gynecology (http://www.abog.org).

New physicians are required to take an examination to be licensed to practice. Every state requires such an examination. It is conducted through the board of medical examiners in each state.

Other Requirements

Oncologists must be extremely hard working, perceptive, and emotionally balanced. They must also be voracious readers to keep up with the new information about the cause, prevention, and treatment of cancer that is updated constantly. Staying current with new information also requires a proficiency with technology because oncologists must use computers to research new developments. They also need research and writing skills to publish their research findings.

In addition to the intellectual rigors of the job, oncologists must be prepared to accept emotional and psychological challenges. Each day, they interact with people who are very ill and frightened. They must be able to maintain objectivity and composure under intensely emotional circumstances. Because oncologists must explain very complex information to patients and their families who may have little or no scientific background, they also must be able to communicate clearly and directly. Excellent interpersonal skills will help the oncologist work as part of a medical team. A surgical oncologist, for example, may have to work with a medical team that includes a dietitian, a physical therapist, the original referring doctor, nurses, and other staff members.

EARNINGS

First-year medical interns earned $47,458 in 2009, according to the Association of American Medical Colleges. Salaries for oncologists in their first year of practice ranged from $120,000 to $215,000, according to Physicians Search, a physician recruitment agency. Those in practice three years or more reported annual earnings of $155,475 to $473,000, with median earnings of $269,298. Individual earnings of oncologists will vary, depending on such factors as geographic location, years of experience, professional reputation, and type of oncology practiced. Fringe benefits for oncologists typically include health and dental insurance, paid vacations, and retirement plans. Self-employed oncologists must provide their own benefits.

OUTLOOK

According to the *Occupational Outlook Handbook*, employment of physicians is expected to grow much faster than the average for all occupations through 2018 due to continued expansion of the health care industry. The specialty of oncology should see strong growth in response to patient demand for access to specialty care. Due to a growing and aging population, increasing numbers of people who survive cancer, new research, changing diagnostic techniques, and new treatment possibilities, oncologists will have many opportunities for employment. The number of physicians who choose to specialize in oncology is slowing. The American Society of Clinical Oncology predicts that there will be a shortage of 2,550 to 4,080 oncologists by 2020.

FOR MORE INFORMATION

For information on certification, contact
American Board of Internal Medicine
510 Walnut Street, Suite 1700
Philadelphia, PA 19106-3699
Tel: 800-441-2246
http://www.abim.org

For general information on various types of cancer, including causes and tips for prevention, contact
American Cancer Society
Tel: 800-227-2345
http://www.cancer.org

For information on careers and news in oncology, contact
American Society of Clinical Oncology
2318 Mill Road, Suite 800
Alexandria, VA 22314-6834
Tel: 571-483-1300
http://www.asco.org

For information on current research and clinical investigations, contact
Radiation Therapy Oncology Group
1818 Market Street, Suite 1600
Philadelphia, PA 19103-3609
Tel: 800-227-5463, ext. 4189
http://www.rtog.org

Ophthalmologists

QUICK FACTS

School Subjects
Biology
Health

Personal Skills
Helping/teaching
Technical/scientific

Work Environment
Primarily indoors
Primarily multiple locations

Minimum Education Level
Medical degree

Salary Range
$120,000 to $256,872 to
$417,000

Certification or Licensing
Required for certain
positions (certification)
Required by all states
(licensing)

Outlook
Much faster than the average

DOT
070

GOE
14.02.01

NOC
3112

O*NET-SOC
29-1067.00, 29-1069.06

OVERVIEW

Ophthalmologists are physicians who specialize in the care of eyes and in the prevention and treatment of eye disease and injury. They test patients' vision and prescribe glasses or contact lenses. Most ophthalmologists also perform eye surgery, treating problems such as cataracts (which cloud vision) and other visual impairments. Because problems with vision may signal larger health problems, ophthalmologists may work with other physicians to help patients deal with diseases such as diabetes or multiple sclerosis. According to the American Medical Association, there are nearly 28,000 ophthalmologists employed in the United States.

HISTORY

Ophthalmology is a medical specialty that dates back to around 1600 B.C., when many vision problems were already recognized. The treatments that were available at the time were primitive, such as using crocodile dung and lizard blood to treat eye problems.

Although the surgeon Susruta performed cataract surgery in India more than 2,000 years ago, Western Europe did not develop the specialty until the mid-1800s. During this era, a solid base of scientific research and medical advances in ophthalmology evolved. The ophthalmoscope, which is an instrument used to view the inside of the eye, was developed during this time.

Ophthalmology has undergone numerous significant scientific and technological breakthroughs in the past decade or so. Using

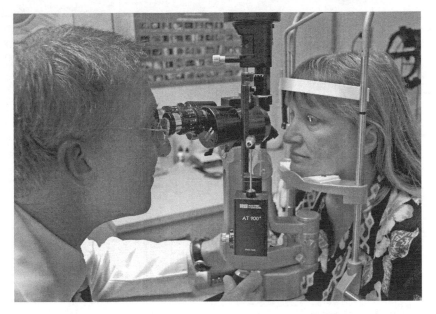

An ophthalmologist examines a patient's eyes. *(David R. Frazier, The Image Works)*

retinal laser surgery (such as LASIK) to correct vision impairments is one recent groundbreaking procedure that has become a common practice among ophthalmologists.

THE JOB

Most ophthalmologists spend four days a week in the office seeing patients and one day a week performing surgery, usually at a hospital. Office visits typically involve performing eye examinations and screening for diseases and infections such as glaucoma and conjunctivitis, or pink eye. Part of the job of ophthalmologists is to prevent vision problems before they start, so many of their patients may have near perfect vision but come in for prevention purposes.

Ophthalmologists treat patients of all ages, from infants to the elderly. During an examination, they check a patient's vision and prescribe glasses and contact lenses to correct any problems. They also screen for diseases using tools such as an ophthalmoscope, which is an instrument used to look at the inside of the eye. When examining a patient's eyes, the ophthalmologist looks for signs of diseases that affect other parts of the body, such as diabetes and hypertension. When such a health problem is discovered, the

Ophthalmological Subspecialties

- Cornea and external disease
- Glaucoma
- Vitreoretinal diseases
- Ophthalmic plastic surgery
- Pediatric ophthalmology
- Neuro-ophthalmology
- Ophthalmic pathology

Visit http://www.aao.org/about/eyemds.cfm to learn more about these subspecialties.

ophthalmologist may work with another physician in diagnosing and managing treatment.

In a typical workweek, an ophthalmologist may see more than 100 patients and perform three or more major surgeries. The most common surgery performed is removing cataracts, which cloud the lens of the eye and cause partial or total blindness. Cataract surgery generally lasts just 30 minutes to an hour and usually helps patients regain all or most of their vision. Some major subspecialties for ophthalmologists include corneal and external disease, glaucoma, pediatric ophthalmology, and ophthalmic pathology.

Ophthalmologists may treat patients who have diseases that could cause them to lose some or all of their vision. That possibility can make patients feel fearful and anxious and can create stress for both the patients and the doctor. For this reason, ophthalmologists need to be able to show patients compassion and understanding in offering their medical expertise.

REQUIREMENTS

High School

To prepare for a career as an ophthalmologist, high school students should enroll in a college preparatory course plan, and take classes in English, languages (especially Latin), the humanities, social studies, foreign language, and mathematics, in addition to courses in biology, chemistry, and physics.

Postsecondary Training

There is often confusion over the difference between an ophthalmologist and an optometrist. Ophthalmologists have medical degrees, while optometrists do not. After earning an M.D. or D.O. degree and becoming licensed to practice medicine (see "Physicians" and "Osteopathic Physicians"), ophthalmologists complete at least one year of general clinical training and at least three years in an eye residency program at a hospital. Often ophthalmologists work at least one more year in a subspecialty fellowship.

Certification or Licensing

To qualify for certification by the American Board of Ophthalmology (ABO) a candidate must successfully complete an ophthalmology course of education and pass written and oral examinations given by the ABO. The ophthalmologist must then complete continuing education requirements and Web-based self-review tests to maintain his or her certification. While certification is voluntary, it is highly recommended. Most hospitals will not grant privileges to an ophthalmologist without board certification. Health maintenance organizations and other insurance groups will not make referrals or payments without certification.

Licensing is mandatory in the United States. It is required in all states before any doctor can practice medicine. In order to be licensed, doctors must graduate from medical school, pass the licensing test of the state in which they will practice, and complete a residency. Physicians licensed in one state can usually get licensed to practice in another state without further testing, however, some states may limit reciprocity.

Other Requirements

Without good motor skills, depth perception, and color vision, an ophthalmologist may have trouble using instruments that are part of the practice. In addition, ophthalmologists need to be patient and good at communicating with people in order to work with patients and other doctors.

EARNINGS

Ophthalmologists' salaries vary by the size of the hospital or health care facility where they work and the city or town where they practice. Other factors affecting salary include the ophthalmologist's practice, hours worked per week, and professional reputation. According to Physicians Search, a physician recruitment agency, average starting salaries for ophthalmologists ranged from $120,000 to $190,000 in 2009. Ophthalmologists in practice for three years or more earned salaries that ranged from $161,763 to $417,000, with an average of $256,872.

Benefits for full-time workers include vacation and sick time, health, and sometimes dental, insurance, and pension or 401(k) plans. Self-employed ophthalmologists must provide their own benefits.

WORK ENVIRONMENT

The offices and examining rooms of most ophthalmologists are well equipped, attractive, well lighted, and well ventilated. There is usually at least one nurse-receptionist on the ophthalmologist's staff, and there may be several nurses, a laboratory technician, one or more secretaries, a bookkeeper, or receptionist.

Ophthalmologists usually see patients by appointments that are scheduled according to individual requirements. They may reserve all mornings for hospital visits and surgery. They may see patients in the office only on certain days of the week.

Ophthalmologists in academic medicine or in research have regular hours, work under good physical conditions, and often determine their own workload. Teaching and research ophthalmologists alike are usually provided with the best and most modern equipment.

OUTLOOK

Employment for physicians is projected to grow much faster than the average for all careers through 2018, according to the *Occupational Outlook Handbook*. The demand for specialty care will provide many job opportunities for ophthalmologists and other specialists. The increasing number of elderly people will drive demand for vision care. Also, new technology (such as a wider use of lasers to correct vision problems) will allow doctors to treat and detect vision disease and impairments that were previously treatable by invasive surgery or eyewear.

FOR MORE INFORMATION

For information on careers and residency programs, contact
  American Academy of Ophthalmology
  PO Box 7424
  San Francisco, CA 94120-7424

Tel: 415-561-8500
http://www.aao.org

For information on certification, contact
American Board of Ophthalmology
111 Presidential Boulevard, Suite 241
Bala Cynwyd, PA 19004-1075
Tel: 610-664-1175
E-mail: info@abop.org
http://www.abop.org

For information on education and careers in the field, visit
Envision Ophthalmology
http://www.aao.org/aao/careers/envision

Osteopathic Physicians

OVERVIEW

Doctors of Osteopathic Medicine (D.O.s), sometimes referred to as *osteopaths*, practice a medical discipline that uses refined and sophisticated manipulative therapy based on the late 19th century teachings of American Dr. Andrew Taylor Still. It embraces the idea of "whole person" medicine and looks upon the system of muscles, bones, and joints—particularly the spine—as reflecting the body's diseases and as being partially responsible for initiating disease processes. Osteopathic physicians are medical doctors with additional specialized training in this unique approach. They practice in a wide range of fields, from environmental medicine, geriatrics, and nutrition to sports medicine and neurology, among others. Approximately 40,000 osteopathic physicians are members of the American Osteopathic Association and an estimated 60,000 D.O.s are in active practice.

HISTORY

Osteopathic medicine has its roots in the hardships and challenges of 19th-century America. Its developer, Dr. Andrew Taylor Still, was born in 1828 in Virginia, the son of a Methodist minister and physician. There were few medical schools in the United States, so Still received his early medical training largely from his father. As the Civil War began, he attended the College of Physicians and Surgeons in Kansas City, but he enlisted in the army before completing the course.

In 1864, an epidemic of meningitis struck the Missouri frontier. Thousands died, including Still's three children. His inability to help them underscored his growing dissatisfaction with traditional medical approaches. After much careful study of anatomy, physiology, and the general nature of health, he became convinced that cultivating a deep understanding of the structure-function relationship between the parts of the body was the only path to a true understanding of disease. Eventually, Still came to believe in three basic principles that would form the core of his osteopathic approach to the practice of medicine. First, he saw the body as capable of self-healing, producing its own healing substances. Second, he felt health was dependent upon the structural integrity of the body. And, finally, because of these beliefs, he considered distorted structure a fundamental cause of disease.

A system of physical manipulation was an integral component of Still's new practice. He began to compare manipulative therapy with other methods then used by doctors, such as drugs and surgery. Often, he found the use of manipulative methods made drugs and operations unnecessary. Instead, he focused on the musculoskeletal system—the muscles, bones, nerves, and ligaments. Recognizing that structural misalignments often occurred in these areas, he emphasized the system's importance as a major potential factor in disease, ripe for the application of his new manipulative techniques.

Still founded the first college of osteopathic medicine in Kirksville, Missouri, in 1892, basing it upon the fundamental principles of his osteopathic concept. Fewer than 20 men and women graduated from this first osteopathic medical college in 1894. Today, there are 25 osteopathic medical schools in the United States. Some are part of major university campuses, and combined, they accept roughly 4,400 new osteopathic students annually.

Still died in 1917, leaving behind a legacy of enormous importance to the history of medicine. Medicine as we know it was in its infancy in his day, and theories, tools, and techniques we take for granted now—such as the concept of germs, the use of antiseptics, and the diagnostic possibilities presented by radiology—were just beginning. In this challenging environment, Still worked out a practical system of structural therapeutics that has withstood the pressure of later discoveries.

Although practitioners of alternative methods of healing in the United States were—and sometimes still are—seen as a threat by the medical profession, osteopathic medicine has increased in popularity. As the field grew, some students wished to use drugs as well as osteopathic techniques in treating patients. John Martin Littlejohn, for

Facts About Osteopathic Medicine

- About 55 percent of osteopathic physicians specialize in the primary care areas of family medicine, internal medicine, pediatrics, and obstetrics/gynecology.

- Approximately 7 percent of physicians in the United States were trained at osteopathic medical colleges.

- Osteopathic physicians are responsible for 16 percent of patient visits in communities with fewer than 2,500 people.

- The number of osteopathic physicians is expected to grow rapidly in coming years. By 2020, it is predicted that there will be at least 100,000 osteopathic physicians practicing in the United States.

- Osteopathic physicians have served as the surgeon general of the U.S. Army and the administrator of the National Highway Traffic Safety Administration.

Source: American Osteopathic Association

example—a Scotsman who studied with Still—widened the focus of osteopathy by concentrating not only on anatomy, but stressing physiological aspects as well. Unlike Still, Littlejohn wanted osteopathic physicians to learn all about modern medicine, along with osteopathic principles and practices. Later, Littlejohn returned to Britain, where he founded the British School of Osteopathy. Even so, the training of osteopathic physicians in the United States was, in fact, eventually to merge with the training of orthodox medical physicians.

THE JOB

Osteopathic and orthodox medicine both use the scientific knowledge of anatomy and physiology, as well as clinical methods of investigation. In this respect, they have a similar language. The greatest differences, however, lie in the way patients are evaluated and in the approach to treatment. As a general rule, the orthodox medical approach focuses on the end result of the problem: the illness. Treatments seek to repair the imbalance presented by the illness through the prescription of drugs or by surgery. In contrast, osteopathic physicians focus on tracing the changes in a patient's ability to function that have occurred over a period of time. This is done to understand the chain of events that have altered the relationship between structure and function, resulting in the patient's present complaint. The primary aim of treatment is to remove the obstacles within a patient's body that are preventing the natural self-healing process from occurring. It's a subtle difference, but important.

Like most physicians, osteopaths spend much of their day seeing patients in a clinic or hospital setting. Their specialty, of course, may take them to other venues, such as nursing homes or sports arenas.

The osteopathic physician's first task in evaluating a new patient is trying to understand the cause of the problem that the patient presents. It may sound simple, but it can be very complex. Diagnosis is a fluid art, and treatment programs are reviewed with each patient visit, changing as the patient begins to respond. To arrive at an appropriate diagnosis, osteopathic physicians record and analyze the history of prior treatment. This report will likely be greatly detailed, since osteopathic physicians consider the whole body. Since structure and function are interdependent, and all the parts of the body connect with each other, osteopaths ask questions that appear to have little relevance to the problem at hand. It is precisely that concern for seemingly irrelevant details, coupled with manipulative therapy, which distinguishes the osteopath from the more conventional Doctor of Medicine (M.D.)

One technique that assists in the correct evaluation of patient problems is palpation, a manual means of diagnosis and determination, whereby sensory information is received through the fingers and hands. Along with careful listening and observation, osteopathic physicians use palpation to assess healthy tissue and identify structural problems or painful areas in a patient's body.

The osteopathic physician differs from a traditional M.D., or *allopathic physician*, in one other major aspect: treatment options. For the osteopathic physician, treatment centers on what are called osteopathic lesions, which are functional disturbances in the body that may involve muscles, joints, and other body systems. These lesions are created by mechanical and physiological reactions in the body to various types of trauma. In osteopathy, open, unhindered, and balanced movement is the most important factor in health. The lack of balance plays a major role in the onset of disease and illness. Thus, the many varied techniques employed by osteopathic physicians are concerned primarily with reestablishing normal mobility and removing or reducing the underlying lesions.

The techniques available to treat osteopathic lesions are nearly limitless. Because osteopathic physicians consider the whole body when determining the proper treatment, each application of a particular technique will be unique. Similar lesions in different patients will have different origins and will have been caused by different sorts of forces or events. Thorough evaluation of the patient help guide osteopaths in discerning what sorts of techniques will be most helpful.

REQUIREMENTS

High School
Students who plan a career as a physician, either as a D.O. or an M.D., should take a college preparatory program in high school. You'll need a strong foundation in the sciences, especially biology, chemistry, and physics. In addition, take English, history, foreign languages, and all the math you can. Psychology is a helpful course in preparing you to work well with a wide variety of people coming to you for treatment. Strive to become as well rounded an individual as possible.

Postsecondary Training
After obtaining a bachelor's degree, prospective osteopathic physicians must apply to medical school. Students file applications along with their college transcripts and MCAT (Medical College Admission Test) scores. Admission to an osteopathic medical school, like all medical schools, is quite competitive.

The academic program leading to the Doctor of Osteopathic Medicine degree involves four years of study, followed by a one-year rotating internship in areas such as internal medicine, obstetrics/gynecology, and surgery. Those interested in a specific specialty must complete an additional two to six years of residency training.

The curriculum in colleges of osteopathic medicine supports Still's osteopathic philosophy, with an emphasis on preventive, family, and community medicine. Clinical instruction stresses examining all patient characteristics (including behavioral and environmental) and how various body systems interrelate. Close attention is given to the ways in which the musculoskeletal and nervous systems influence the functioning of the entire body. An increasing emphasis on biomedical research in several of the colleges has expanded opportunities for students wishing to pursue research careers.

Certification or Licensing
The American Osteopathic Association (AOA) offers board certification, which entails passing a comprehensive written exam as a well as a practical test demonstrating osteopathic manipulative techniques. The AOA offers specialty certification in 18 areas. To retain certification, physicians must complete 120 hours of continuing education

within a three-year period. Continuing education can be acquired in a variety of ways, including attending professional conferences, completing education programs sponsored by the AOA, teaching osteopathic medicine, and publishing articles in professional journals. Some osteopathic physicians are certified by both the AOA and the American Medical Association.

At an early point in the residency period, all physicians, both M.D.s and D.O.s, must pass a state medical board examination in order to obtain a license and enter practice. Each state sets its own requirements and issues its own licenses, although some states will accept licenses from other states.

Other Requirements

The practice of osteopathic medicine usually involves a lot of personal interaction and a lot of touching, which can make some patients—and some prospective doctors—feel uncomfortable. If you plan to become an osteopathic physician, you will need excellent communication skills to tell patients what to expect and what is happening at any one moment. If patients don't understand what you are telling them, they may not pursue treatment. For this reason, good communication skills are crucial. You will also need to learn to work well with others and to be a perceptive listener.

Since a large number of osteopathic physicians go into private practice, business and management skills are useful. In addition, good manual dexterity is important. Finally, and most importantly, you must have a real commitment to caring for people in this medically specialized way.

EXPLORING

Consider visiting an osteopathic medical college. Tours are often available and can give you extra insight into necessary training and the ways in which life at an osteopathic medical school differs from a "regular" one. If you don't live close enough to an osteopathic college to visit, write for more information or visit its Web site.

Check into after-school or summer jobs at your local hospital or medical center. Any job that exposes you to the care of patients is a good one, even jobs you might not think of at first, or ones that aren't exactly medical, such as working with the janitorial service. Contact the American Osteopathic Association and ask for a list of osteopathic physicians in your area. Talk to as many people as you can, and don't be afraid to ask questions.

EMPLOYERS

Osteopathic physicians can be found in virtually all medical specialties. More than one-third of all osteopathic physicians go into private practice after completing their training. They also work in hospitals, clinics, nursing homes, and other health care settings. Approximately 40,000 osteopaths are members of the American Osteopathic Association and about 60,000 D.O.s are in active practice.

STARTING OUT

Depending on the specialty in which an osteopathic physician is interested, he or she can plan on completing a residency program of two to seven years' duration. One of the difficulties facing the profession today is that medical schools produce more students than there are available residencies at osteopathic hospitals. As a result, gaining admission to selective osteopathic medicine programs may be challenging. Graduates increasingly find residencies in traditional medical facilities. As awareness of and interest in osteopathic medicine continue to grow, this shortage of open residency positions may change. After completing a residency program, an osteopathic physician can choose to go into private practice or explore positions with a variety of health care employers.

ADVANCEMENT

Advancement in the medical professions is dependent on the specific field. Osteopathic physicians in private practice will follow a different career path than those working in a purely clinical setting or in a research position at an academic medical center. As noted earlier, a large percentage of osteopathic physicians go into private or small-group practice. Advancement in private practice comes with increased reputation; mainly through word of mouth, a practice grows with positive referrals.

In contrast, osteopathic physicians in employee positions are more limited in their methods of advancement. Those in an academic setting face the challenge of obtaining tenure to advance from instructor to assistant professor to associate professor to full professor. Becoming tenured is an arduous process, involving a combination of patient care, research, publication, and administrative responsibilities. Those who love the academic environment, however, and also want to be a practicing physician usually find their niche in academia.

EARNINGS

Osteopathic physicians earn incomes comparable to their M.D. counterparts. The potentially high income that comes with becoming established as a physician can be an enticing perk. According to the U.S. Department of Labor, physicians not otherwise classified earned mean annual salaries of $173,860 in 2009. Those employed in offices of physicians earned mean annual salaries of $202,480. A 2010 salary survey by Payscale.com reported salaries for osteopathic physicians ranged from less than $98,264 to $274,689 or more, depending on their area of practice. There are a number of other factors to keep in mind when considering salary, however. Counting postgraduate education, most physicians are in their early 30s before starting to practice. Residency pay is low (medical residents averaged $47,458 a year in 2009), yet residents work up to 80 hours per week. Most physicians incur high educational debt by the time they begin to practice.

Benefits for osteopathic physicians vary, depending on whether they work in private practice or for an employer. A survey by the American Medical Association indicates that median net income for self-employed physicians is approximately 40 percent higher than that of employee physicians. Many factors contribute to the difference. Self-employed physicians tend to be older, have more years of experience, work more hours, and be more likely to be board certified, all of which are associated with higher earnings. On the other hand, 75 percent of employee physicians receive noncash benefits in addition to their reported income, whereas some self-employed physicians do not. These benefits represent approximately 5 percent of income for employees.

WORK ENVIRONMENT

As with the benefits earned, the environment in which an osteopathic physician works can vary. In private practice and employer-based situations, osteopathic physicians work both alone (directly with a patient) and as part of a team. Osteopathic medicine, like all medical professions, is a field of contrasts, requiring both collaboration and personal insight. The primary obstacle to be aware of going into almost any field of medicine is long hours and erratic schedules, particularly during training.

OUTLOOK

According to the American Association of Colleges of Osteopathic Medicine (AACOM), the number of osteopathic medicine graduates has increased approximately 37 percent since 1998, making osteopathic medicine one of the fastest-growing health professions in the country. Nearly one in five medical students in the United States attend an osteopathic medical school, according to the AACOM. To meet the growing demand, more than a dozen new osteopathic medical colleges have opened their doors since the mid-1970s. Together, all 25 institutions currently enroll more than 16,800 students annually, of whom nearly 50 percent are women.

Although osteopathic medicine is not strictly an "alternative" approach, the field is benefiting from the current interest in these kinds of therapy. Excellent job opportunities will continue to become available for skilled osteopathic physicians. In addition to specialized practices in areas such as family medicine, increasing interest in biomedical research at the osteopathic colleges also is expanding opportunities for candidates interested in careers in medical research.

FOR MORE INFORMATION

To read the Osteopathic Medical College Information Book *and for information on financial aid, visit the Web site of the AACOM.*
American Association of Colleges of Osteopathic Medicine (AACOM)
5550 Friendship Boulevard, Suite 310
Chevy Chase, MD 20815-7231
Tel: 301-968-4100
http://www.aacom.org

For information on osteopathic medicine, visit the AOA Web site.
American Osteopathic Association (AOA)
142 East Ontario Street
Chicago, IL 60611-2874
Tel: 800-621-1773
http://www.osteopathic.org

Pathologists

OVERVIEW

Pathologists are physicians who analyze tissue specimens to identify abnormalities and diagnose diseases.

HISTORY

During the late Middle Ages, the earliest known autopsies were performed to determine cause of death in humans. As these autopsies were documented, much information about human anatomy was gathered and studied. In 1761, the culmination of autopsy material resulted in the first textbook of anatomy by Giovanni Battista Morgagni, who is known today as the "father of pathology."

Many developments in pathology occurred during the 19th century, including the discovery of the relationship between clinical symptoms and pathological changes. By the mid-1800s, Rudolf Virchow had established the fact that cells, of which all things are composed, are produced by other living cells. He became known as the founder of cellular pathology. Louis Pasteur and Robert Koch later developed the bacteriologic theory, which was fundamental to understanding disease processes. By the late 19th century, pathology was a recognized medical specialty.

Technological advances in the 20th and early 21st century, from electron microscopes to computers, have led to further growth and developments in the field of pathology.

QUICK FACTS

School Subjects
Biology
Health

Personal Skills
Helping/teaching
Technical/scientific

Work Environment
Primarily indoors
Primarily multiple locations

Minimum Education Level
Medical degree

Salary Range
$194,372 to $240,414 to
$276,829+

Certification or Licensing
Required for certain
positions (certification)
Required by all states
(licensing)

Outlook
Much faster than the average

DOT
070

GOE
14.01.01

NOC
3112

O*NET-SOC
29-1069.07

THE JOB

Pathologists provide information that helps physicians care for patients; because of this, the pathologist is sometimes called the "doctor's doctor." When a patient has a tumor, an infection, or symptoms of a disease, a pathologist examines tissues from the patient to determine the nature of the patient's condition. Without this knowledge, a physician would not be able to make an accurate diagnosis and design the appropriate treatment. Because many health conditions first manifest themselves at the cellular level, pathologists are often able to identify conditions before they turn into serious health problems.

Many people associate pathologists only with the performing of autopsies. In fact, while pathologists do perform autopsies, much of their work involves living patients. Pathologists working in hospital laboratories examine the blood, urine, bone marrow, stools, tissues, and tumors of patients. Using a variety of techniques, pathologists locate the causes of infections and determine the nature of unusual growths. Pathologists consult with a patient's physician to determine the best course of treatment. They may also talk with the patient

Pathology Subspecialties

- Cardiovascular pathology: heart and blood vessels
- Cytopathology: cells
- Dermatopathology: skin
- Environmental pathology: disease caused by environmental factors
- Gastrointestinal pathology: stomach and digestive tract
- Gynecologic/obstetrical pathology: female reproductive system and childbirth
- Hematopathology: blood
- Immunopatholgy: immune system
- Neuropathology: nervous system
- Ophthalmic pathology: eyes
- Pediatric pathology: children
- Pulmonary pathology: lungs
- Renal pathology: kidneys

about his or her condition. In a sense, the work of pathologists is much like detective work. It is often through the efforts of pathologists that health conditions are recognized and properly treated.

Forensic pathologists are specialists who typically examine the deceased (usually those who die unexpectedly, suddenly, or violently) to determine cause and manner of death.

REQUIREMENTS

High School

If you are interested in pursuing a medical degree, a high school education emphasizing college preparatory classes is a must. Science courses, such as biology, chemistry, and physics are necessary, as are math courses (such as algebra, geometry, and calculus). These classes will not only provide you with an introduction to basic science and math concepts, but also allow you to determine your own aptitude in these areas. Especially important are any courses emphasizing laboratory work. Since college will be your next educational step, it is also important to take English courses to develop your researching and writing skills. Foreign language and social science classes will also help make you an appealing candidate for college admission as well as prepare you for your future undergraduate and graduate education. Courses in computer science are a must as well.

Postsecondary Training

Like any medical specialist, a pathologist must earn an M.D. or D.O. degree and become licensed to practice medicine (see "Physicians" and "Osteopathic Physicians"), after which begins a four-year pathology residency. Residents may choose to specialize in anatomical pathology (AP) or clinical pathology (CP). Many pathologists, however, prefer to specialize in both anatomical and clinical pathology; licensing as an AP/CP pathologist requires a five-year residency. Various subspecialties require further training beyond the residency. Visit http://www.pathologytraining.org for a searchable database of pathology training programs in the United States and Canada.

Certification or Licensing

All physicians must be licensed to practice medicine. The American Board of Pathology is the governing board for pathologist certification. A pathologist can pursue certification along three primary paths—an anatomical pathology program, a clinical pathology program, or a combined anatomical and clinical pathology program. Once a pathologist has completed certification, he or she can choose to earn subspecialty certification in a particular area of pathology. Gaining certification in a specialty generally requires an additional one to two years of training, although there is a potential for combining this training with the standard pathology residency program.

Other Requirements
Successful pathologists should have an eye for detail and be able to concentrate intently on work, work well and communicate effectively with others, and be able to accept a great deal of responsibility. They need to perform well under pressure, be patient, thorough, and confident in decisions.

EARNINGS
First-year medical interns earned $47,458 in 2009, according to the Association of American Medical Colleges. Pathologists earned a median annual salary of $240,414 in November 2009, according to Salary.com. Salaries for pathologists ranged from less than $194,372 to $276,829 or more. Several factors influence earnings, including years of experience, geographic region of practice, and reputation.

Pathologists who work for laboratories, hospitals, and other employers usually receive benefits such as vacation days, sick leave, health and life insurance, and a savings and pension program. Self-employed pathologists must provide their own benefits.

WORK ENVIRONMENT
The offices and laboratories of most pathologists are well equipped, attractive, well lighted, and well ventilated. Although pathologists do not have much direct patient contact, they do have a lot of contact with physicians and clinical staff. In addition to their medical duties, pathologists who are self-employed or who are in a small group practice must focus on business aspects such as paperwork, supervising staff, and marketing their services.

OUTLOOK
Employment for physicians is expected to grow much faster than the average for all careers through 2018, according to the U.S. Department of Labor. The outlook for careers in pathology is especially strong. New medical tests are constantly being developed and

refined, making it possible to detect an increasing number of diseases in their early stages. The medical community depends on pathologists to analyze results from these tests. Another factor favorably affecting the demand for pathologists is the shifting of health care to cost-consciousness managed care services. Testing for, diagnosing, and treating a disease or other health condition in its early stages is much less expensive than treating a health condition in its advanced stages.

FOR MORE INFORMATION

For information on certification, contact
American Board of Pathology
PO Box 25915
Tampa, FL 33622-5915
Tel: 813-286-2444
E-mail: questions@abpath.org
http://www.abpath.org

For information on pathology careers, contact
American Society for Clinical Pathology
33 West Monroe Street, Suite 1600
Chicago, IL 60603-5308
Tel: 800-267-2727
E-mail: info@ascp.org
http://www.ascp.org

Visit the society's Web site for information on training programs and to read Pathology as a Career in Medicine.
American Society for Investigative Pathology
9650 Rockville Pike, Suite E133
Bethesda, MD 20814-3993
Tel: 301-634-7130
E-mail: asip@asip.org
http://www.asip.org

For information on pathology for practitioners and the general public, contact
College of American Pathologists
325 Waukegan Road
Northfield, IL 60093-2750
Tel: 800-323-4040
http://www.cap.org

For information on pathology training programs in the United States and Canada, contact
   The Intersociety Committee on Pathology Information
   9650 Rockville Pike
   Bethesda, MD 20814-3993
   Tel: 301-634-7200
   E-mail: ICPI@asip.org
   http://www.pathologytraining.org

For comprehensive information on the career of forensic patholo-gist, visit the association's Web site.
   National Association of Medical Examiners
   31479 Arrow Lane
   Marceline, MO 64658-7300
   Tel: 660-734-1891
   E-mail: name@thename.org
   http://www.thename.org

For information on membership, contact
   United States and Canadian Academy of Pathology
   3643 Walton Way Extension
   Augusta, GA 30909-4507
   Tel: 706-733-7550
   http://www.uscap.org

Pediatricians

OVERVIEW

Pediatricians are physicians who provide health care to infants, children, and adolescents. Typically, a pediatrician meets a new patient soon after birth and takes care of that patient through his or her teenage years. There are more than 29,000 pediatricians employed in the United States.

HISTORY

Children became the focus of separate medical care during the 18th century in Europe. Children's health care became a recognized medical specialty during the early 19th century, and by the middle of the 19th century, pediatrics was taught separately in medical schools. The first pediatric clinic in the United States opened in New York City in 1862. About that same time, several children's hospitals opened in Europe.

Studies focused on developing treatments for infectious diseases of childhood such as measles and scarlet fever. By the beginning of the 20th century, pediatricians began promoting the normal growth and development of children. Well-child clinics began to open around the United States.

Some of the most significant breakthroughs in children's health care have been in disease prevention. By the middle of the 20th century, the development of vaccines and antibiotics greatly decreased the threat of infectious diseases.

Books to Read

Behrman, Richard E., Robert Kliegman, Hal B. Jenson, and James T. Cassidy. (eds.) *Nelson Textbook of Pediatrics.* 18th ed. Philadelphia: W. B. Saunders, 2007.

Hay, William W., Myron J. Levin, Judith M. Sondheimer, and Robin R. Deterding. *Current Pediatric Diagnosis and Treatment.* 19th ed. New York: McGraw-Hill, 2008.

Klass, Perri. *The Real Life of a Pediatrician.* New York: Kaplan Publishing, 2009.

McCarthy, Claire. *Everyone's Child: A Pediatrician's Story of an Inner-City Practice.* New York: Scribner, 2002.

Polin, Richard A., and Mark F. Ditmar. (eds.) *Pediatric Secrets.* 4th ed. St. Louis: Mosby, 2005.

THE JOB

A significant part of a pediatrician's job is preventive medicine—what is sometimes called "well care." This involves periodically seeing a patient for routine health checkups. During these checkups, the doctor physically examines the child to make sure he or she is growing at a normal rate and to look for symptoms of illness. The physical examination includes testing reflexes, listening to the heart and lungs, checking eyes and ears, and measuring height and weight.

During the checkup, the pediatrician also assesses the child's mental and behavioral development. This is done both by observing the patient's behavior and by asking the parents questions about their child's abilities.

Immunizing children against certain childhood diseases is another important part of preventive medicine. Pediatricians administer routine immunizations for such diseases as rubella, polio, and smallpox as children reach certain ages. Yet another part of preventive medicine is family education. Pediatricians counsel and advise parents on the care and treatment of their children. They provide information on such parental concerns as safety, diet, and hygiene.

In addition to practicing preventive medicine, pediatricians also treat sick infants and children. When a sick or injured patient is brought into the office, the doctor examines him or her, makes a diagnosis, and orders treatment. Common ailments include ear infections, allergies, feeding difficulties, viral illnesses, respiratory illnesses, and gastrointestinal upsets. For these and other illnesses, pediatricians prescribe and administer treatments and medications.

If a patient is seriously ill or hurt, a pediatrician arranges for hospital admission and follows up on the patient's progress during the hospitalization. In some cases, a child may have a serious condition, such as cancer, cystic fibrosis, or hemophilia, that requires the attention of a specialist. In these cases, the pediatrician, as the primary care physician, will refer the child to the appropriate specialist.

Some pediatric patients may be suffering from emotional or behavioral disorders or from substance abuse. Other patients may be affected by problems within their families, such as unemployment, alcoholism, or physical abuse. In these cases, pediatricians may make referrals to such health professionals as psychiatrists, psychologists, and social workers.

Some pediatricians choose to pursue pediatric subspecialties, such as the treatment of children who have heart disorders, kidney disorders, or cancer. Subspecialization requires a longer residency training than does general practice. A pediatrician practicing a subspecialty typically spends a much greater proportion of his or her time in a hospital or medical center than does a general practice pediatrician. Subspecialization permits pediatricians to be involved in research activities.

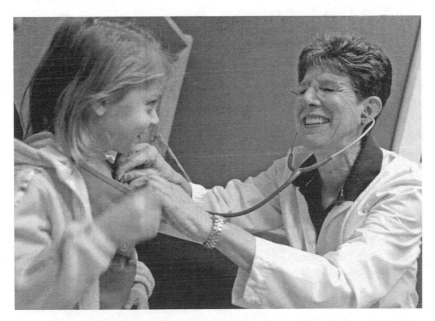

A pediatrician listens to a young girl's heartbeat. *(Patrick Dove, AP Photo)*

REQUIREMENTS

High School

While in high school, take college preparatory classes, with a heavy emphasis on science and math. Biology, chemistry, physics, and physiology are important science classes. Any advanced math courses are also excellent choices.

Classes in English, foreign languages, and speech will enhance communication skills, which are vital to being a successful physician. Social sciences such as psychology and sociology, which increase your understanding of others, are also beneficial.

Postsecondary Training

After earning an M.D. or D.O. degree and becoming licensed to practice medicine (see "Physicians" and "Osteopathic Physicians"), pediatricians must complete a three-year residency program in a hospital. The pediatric residency provides extensive experience in ambulatory pediatrics, the care of infants and children who are not bedridden. Residents also spend time working in various specialized pediatric units, including neonatology, adolescent medicine, child development, psychology, special care, intensive care, and outpatient.

Some of the other subspecialties a pediatrician might acquire training for include adolescent medicine, *pediatric cardiology* (care of children with heart disease), *pediatric critical care* (care of children requiring advanced life support), *pediatric endocrinology* (care of children with diabetes and other glandular disorders), *pediatric neurology* (care of children with nervous system disorders), and *pediatric hematology/oncology* (care of children with blood disorders and cancer).

Certification or Licensing

Certification by the American Board of Pediatrics is recommended. A certificate in general pediatrics is awarded after three years of residency training and the successful completion of a comprehensive written examination. A pediatrician who specializes in cardiology, infectious diseases, or other areas must complete an additional three-year residency in the subspecialty before taking the certification examination.

All physicians must be licensed to practice in the United States. To become licensed, physicians must pass a state exam, which is administered by their state's board of medical examiners.

Other Requirements

To be a successful pediatrician, you should like children and adolescents; have patience, compassion, and a good sense of humor; be willing to continually learn; have a desire to help others; and be able to withstand stress and make sound decisions.

EARNINGS

Pediatricians, while at the low end of the earning scale for physicians, still have among the highest earnings of any occupation in the United States.

First-year medical interns earned $47,458 in 2009, according to the Association of American Medical Colleges. According to the U.S. Department of Labor (DOL), pediatricians had median earnings of $152,240 in 2009. The DOL reported salaries for pediatricians ranged from less than $88,840 to $175,940 or more. The earnings of pediatricians are partly dependent upon the types of practices they choose. Those who are self-employed tend to earn more than those who are salaried. Geographic region, hours worked, number of years in practice, professional reputation, and personality are other factors that can impact a pediatrician's income.

Benefits for pediatricians depend on the employer; however, they usually include such items as health insurance, retirement or 401(k) plans, and paid vacation days. Self-employed pediatricians must provide their own benefits.

WORK ENVIRONMENT

Pediatricians in general practice usually work alone or in partnership with other physicians. Their average workweek is 50 to 60 hours, most of which is spent seeing patients in their offices. They also make hospital rounds to visit any of their patients who have been admitted for treatment or to check on newborn patients and their mothers. Pediatricians spend some time on call, taking care of patients who have emergencies. A pediatrician might be called to attend the delivery of a baby, to meet an injured patient in the emergency room, or simply to answer a parent's question about a sick child.

Some pediatricians choose to pursue pediatric subspecialties, such as the treatment of children who have heart disorders, kidney disorders, or cancer. Subspecialization requires a longer residency training than does general practice. A pediatrician practicing a subspecialty typically spends a much greater proportion of his or her time in a hospital or medical center than does a general practice pediatrician. Subspecialization permits pediatricians to be involved in research activities.

OUTLOOK

Employment for physicians is expected to grow much faster than the average for all careers through 2018, according to the U.S. Department of Labor. The employment prospects for pediatricians—along with other general practitioners, such as family physicians—are especially good. This is because of the increasing use of managed care plans that stress preventive care.

FOR MORE INFORMATION

For general information about the field, contact
Ambulatory Pediatric Association
6728 Old McLean Village Drive
McLean, VA 22101-3906
Tel: 703-556-9222
E-mail: info@academicpeds.org
http://www.ambpeds.org

Visit the academy's Web site to read Pediatrics 101.
American Academy of Pediatrics
141 Northwest Point Boulevard
Elk Grove Village, IL 60007-1019
Tel: 847-434-4000
http://www.aap.org

For information about certification, contact
American Board of Pediatrics
111 Silver Cedar Court
Chapel Hill, NC 27514-1692
Tel: 919-929-0461
E-mail: abpeds@abpeds.org
https://www.abp.org

For information on programs for college students, contact
American Pediatric Society/Society for Pediatric Research
3400 Research Forest Drive, Suite B-7
The Woodlands, TX 77381-4259
Tel: 281-419-0052
E-mail: info@aps-spr.org
http://www.aps-spr.org

Physicians

OVERVIEW

Physicians diagnose, prescribe medicines for, and otherwise treat diseases and disorders of the human body. A physician may also perform surgery and often specializes in one aspect of medical care and treatment. Physicians hold either a doctor of medicine (M.D.) or osteopathic medicine (D.O.) degree.

HISTORY

The first great physician was Hippocrates, a Greek who lived almost 2,500 years ago. He developed theories about the practice of medicine and the anatomy of the human body, but Hippocrates is remembered today for a set of medical ethics that still influences medical practice. The oath that he administered to his disciples is still administered to physicians about to start practice. His 87 treatises on medicine, known as the "Hippocratic Collection," are believed to be the first authoritative record of early medical theory and practice. Hippocratic physicians believed in the theory that health was maintained by a proper balance of four "humors" in the body: blood, phlegm, black bile, and yellow bile.

Another Greek physician, Galen, influenced medical thought for more than a thousand years. During the Middle Ages, his works were translated into Arabic and Syriac.

The great civilizations of Egypt, India, and China all developed medical theories of diagnosis and treatment that influenced later cultures of their own countries and those of other countries. The school of medicine at Alexandria, Egypt, for example, incorporated the theories of the ancient Greeks as well as those of the Egyptians. This great medical school flourished and was influential for several hundred years. Research specialists there learned more about human anatomy than had ever been learned before.

The theories and practices of medicine were kept alive almost entirely during the Middle Ages by monks in monasteries. Few new theories were developed during this period, but the medical records of most of the great early civilizations were carefully preserved and copied.

The Renaissance saw a renewal of interest in medical research. Swiss physician Paracelsus publicly burned the writings of Galen and Avicena, signifying a break with the past. Concepts of psychology and psychiatry were introduced by Juan Luis Vives, a Spanish humanist and physician.

In the 17th century English physician William Harvey discovered that the blood, propelled by the pumping action of the heart, circulates through the body. Many inventions in other fields helped the progress of medicine. Anton van Leeuwenhoek, a Dutch lens grinder, made instruments that magnified up to 270 times. He also studied blood circulation and composition, and was the first to see bacteria and protozoans.

During the 18th century the Dutch physician Hermann Boerhaave introduced clinical instruction (teaching at the bedside of patients). Edward Jenner discovered a vaccination against smallpox. Specialization grew rapidly, as did the growth of medical schools, hospitals, and dispensaries.

The 19th century saw advances in more precise instruments, such as the stethoscope, the ophthalmoscope, and X-rays. Doctors began to use anesthetics like ether and nitrous oxide and antiseptics. Knowledge of the cell, digestion, metabolism, and the vasomotor system increased.

Among the recent discoveries and developments have been the identification of four blood types, the discovery of insulin, development of antibiotics, and immunizations such as the polio vaccine. Technological advances have included the electron microscope, pacemakers, ultrasound, heart-lung machines, dialysis machines, and prostheses, to name only a few. Medical research and practice made giant strides toward the relief of human distress and the prolonging of human life. Every day brings new discoveries and the possibility of major breakthroughs in the areas that have long plagued humans.

THE JOB

The greatest number of physicians are in private practice. They see patients by appointment in their offices and examining rooms, and visit patients who are confined to the hospital. In the hospital, they may perform operations or give other kinds of medical treatment. Some physicians also make calls on patients at home if the patient is not able to get to the physician's office or if the illness is an emergency.

Slightly more than 12 percent of physicians are *general practitioners* or *family practitioners*. They see patients of all ages and both sexes and will diagnose and treat those ailments that are not severe enough or unusual enough to require the services of a specialist. When special problems arise, however, the general practitioner will refer the patient to a specialist.

Not all physicians are engaged in private practice. Some are in academic medicine and teach in medical schools or teaching hospitals. Some are engaged only in research. Some are salaried employees of health maintenance organizations or other prepaid health care plans. Some are salaried hospital employees.

Some physicians, often called *medical officers*, are employed by the federal government, in such positions as public health, or in the service of the Department of Veterans Affairs. State and local governments also employ physicians for public health agency work. A large number of physicians serve with the armed forces, both in this country and overseas.

Industrial physicians or *occupational physicians* are employed by large industrial firms for two main reasons: to prevent illnesses that may be caused by certain kinds of work and to treat accidents or illnesses of employees. Although most industrial physicians may roughly be classified as general practitioners because of the wide variety of illnesses that they must recognize and treat, their knowledge must also extend to public health techniques and to understanding such relatively new hazards as radiation and the toxic effects of various chemicals, including insecticides.

A specialized type of *industrial* or *occupational physician* is the *flight surgeon*. Flight surgeons study the effects of high-altitude flying on the physical condition of flight personnel. They place members of the flight staff in special low-pressure and refrigeration chambers that simulate high-altitude conditions and study the reactions on their blood pressure, pulse and respiration rate, and body temperature.

National Youth Leadership Forum

If you are a high school student who is interested in a career in medicine, you might want to check out the National Youth Leadership Forum (NYLF). This organization offers annual forums for high school students interested in a career in medicine. Forums are held in Atlanta, Boston, Chicago, Houston-Galveston, Los Angeles, Philadelphia, San Francisco, and Washington, D.C. Visit the forum's Web site for information on schedule dates. The forums give students an opportunity to gain hands-on experience in medicine by visiting medical schools, research facilities, and hospitals and talking to people in various stages of the medical career path, from first-year medical students to practicing physicians. The NYLF reports the curriculum in its medical forum covers a broad range of topics in medicine, including educational requirements, career options, clinical practice, and current issues facing the profession. Forums are open students in grades nine through 12 with a B+ grade point average. Teachers and counselors recommend students accepted for forums. Students may ask about the program at their school or contact the NYLF themselves. Tuition fees and travel expenses apply, as NYLF is a nonprofit organization, but many students are able to find sponsors in their community. For more information, contact the National Youth Leadership Forum (1919 Gallows Road, Suite 700, Vienna, VA 22182-4007, 703-584-9240, http://www.nylf.org/med/index.cfm).

Another growing specialty is the field of nuclear medicine. Some large hospitals have a nuclear research laboratory, which functions under the direction of a *chief of nuclear medicine*, who coordinates the activities of the lab with other hospital departments and medical personnel. These physicians perform tests using nuclear isotopes and use techniques that let physicians see and understand organs deep within the body.

M.D.s and D.O.s may become specialists in any of the 36 different general medical care specialties, including allergy and immunology, anesthesiology, dermatology, emergency medicine, family medicine, internal medicine, medical genetics, neurology, nuclear medicine, obstetrics and gynecology, ophthalmology, otolaryngology, pathology, pediatrics, physical medicine and rehabilitation, preventive medicine, psychiatry, radiation oncology, radiology, and urology.

REQUIREMENTS

High School

The physician is required to devote many years to study before being admitted to practice. Interested high school students should enroll in a college preparatory course, and take courses in English, languages (especially Latin), the humanities, social studies, and mathematics, in addition to courses in biology, chemistry, and physics.

Postsecondary Training

To begin a career as a physician you need to first enter a liberal arts program in an accredited undergraduate institution. Some colleges offer a premed major, but a good general education with as many science courses as possible and a major in biology or chemistry is considered adequate preparation for the study of medicine. Courses should include physics, biology, inorganic and organic chemistry, English, mathematics, and the social sciences.

College students should begin to apply to medical schools early in their senior year, so it is advisable to begin your research into schools as early as your freshman year. There are 129 accredited schools of medicine and 25 accredited schools of osteopathic medicine in the country. For more information on becoming an M.D., consult a copy of *Medical School Admission Requirements*, available from the Association of American Medical Colleges (http://www.aamc.org/students/applying/msar.htm). Information about becoming a D.O. can be found in the *Osteopathic Medical College Information Book* (http://www.aacom.org). Read carefully the admissions requirements of the several medical schools to which you hope to apply to avoid making mistakes in choosing a graduate program.

Some students may be admitted to medical school after only three years of study in an undergraduate program. There are a few medical schools that award the bachelor's degree at the end of the first year of medical school study. This practice is becoming less common as more students seek admission to medical schools. Most premed students plan to spend four years in an undergraduate program and to receive the bachelor's degree before entering the four-year medical school program.

During your second or third year in college, you should arrange with an adviser to take the Medical College Admission Test (MCAT). This test is given each spring and each fall at certain selected sites. Your adviser should know the date, place, and time; or you may contact the Association of American Medical Colleges. All medical colleges in the United States require this test for admission, and a student's MCAT score is one of the factors that is weighed in the decision to accept or reject any applicant. Because the test does not evaluate medical knowledge, most college students who are enrolled in liberal arts programs should not find it to be unduly difficult.

You are encouraged to apply to at least three institutions to increase your chances of being accepted by one of them. Approximately 44 percent of qualified applicants to medical schools are admitted each year. To facilitate this process, the American Medical College Application Service (AMCAS) will check, copy, and submit applications to the medical schools you specify. More information about this service may be obtained from the AMCAS (http://www.aamc.org/students/amcas), premedical advisers, and medical schools.

In addition to the traditional medical schools, there are several schools of basic medical sciences that enroll medical students for the first two years (preclinical experience) of medical school. They offer a preclinical curriculum to students similar to that which is offered by a regular medical school. At the end of the two-year program, you can then apply to a four-year medical school for the final two years of instruction.

Although high scholarship is a determining factor in admitting a student to a medical school, it is actually only one of the criteria considered. By far the greatest number of successful applicants to medical schools are B students. Because admission is also determined by a number of other factors, including a personal interview, other qualities in addition to a high scholastic average are considered desirable for a prospective physician. High on the list of desirable qualities are emotional stability, integrity, reliability, resourcefulness, and a sense of service.

The average student enters medical school at age 21 or 22. Then you begin another four years of formal schooling. During the first two years of medical school, studies include human anatomy, biochemistry, physiology, pharmacology, psychology, microbiology, pathology, medical ethics, and laws governing medicine. Most instruction in the first two years is given through classroom lectures, laboratories, seminars, independent research, and the reading of textbook material and other types of literature. You also learn to take medical histories, examine patients, and recognize symptoms.

During the last two years in medical school, you become actively involved in the treatment process. You spend a large proportion of the time in the hospital as part of a medical team headed by a teaching physician who specializes in a particular area. Others on the team may be interns or residents. You are closely supervised as you learn techniques such as how to take a patient's medical history, how to conduct a physical examination, how to work in the laboratory, how to make a diagnosis, and how to keep all the necessary records.

As you rotate from one medical specialty to another, you obtain a broad understanding of each field. You are assigned to duty in internal medicine, pediatrics, psychiatry, obstetrics and gynecology, surgery, and other specialties.

In addition to this hospital work, you continue to take course work. You are responsible for assigned studies and also for some independent study.

Most states require all new M.D.s and D.O.s to complete at least one year of postgraduate training, and a few require an internship plus a one-year residency. If you decide to specialize, you will spend from three to seven years in advanced residency training. (The Accreditation Council for Graduate Medical Education offers a list of accredited post–M.D. medical training programs in the United States at its Web site, http://www.acgme.org). Then you must pass a specialty board examination to become a board-certified physician. The residency years are stressful—residents often work 24-hour shifts and put in up to 80 hours per week. Additionally, some physicians who are interested in practicing in a subspecialty, such as gastroenterology, a subspecialty of internal medicine and of pediatrics, participate in fellowships that last one to three years.

For a teaching or research career, you may also earn a master's degree or a Ph.D. in a biology or chemistry subfield, such as biochemistry or microbiology.

Certification or Licensing

After receiving the M.D. or D.O. degree, the new physician is required to take an examination to be licensed to practice. Every state requires such an examination. It is conducted through the board of medical examiners in each state. Some states have reciprocity agreements with other states so that a physician licensed in one state may be automatically licensed in another without being required to pass another examination. This is not true throughout the United States, however, so it is wise to find out about licensing procedures before planning to move. Board certification is also available in a variety of medical specialties. Those seeking to become board certified participate in residencies that last up to seven years and must pass an examination by a member board of the American Board of Medical Specialties or the American Osteopathic Association. Many physicians choose to become certified in their field because certification enables the public to identify practitioners who have met a standard of training and experience beyond the level required for licensure. As consumers become more informed and health care becomes more market-driven, physicians who are board certified are expected to be more in demand. Many patient advocate groups and patient information sources urge patients to choose physicians who are board certified. Most hospitals will not grant privileges to an ophthalmologist without board certification. Health maintenance organizations and other insurance groups will not make referrals or payments without certification.

Other Requirements

You must have some plan for financing your long and costly education. You face a period of at least eight years after college when you will not be self-supporting. While still in school, you may be able to work only during summer vacations, because the necessary laboratory courses of the regular school year are so time consuming that little time is left for activities other than the preparation of daily lessons. Some scholarships and loans are available to qualified students.

If you work directly with patients, you need to have great sensitivity to their needs. Interpersonal skills are important, even in isolated research laboratories, since you must work and communicate with other scientists. Since new technology and discoveries happen at such a rapid rate, you must continually pursue further education to keep up with new treatments, tools, and medicines.

EXPLORING

At the high school and undergraduate levels, you can begin to learn about the field of medicine by volunteering at hospitals, nursing homes, or clinics. By working in these settings you will not only have the opportunity to gauge how much you enjoy this type of work, but you will also have the chance to be around professionals in the field.

Another way you can explore is by talking to medical professionals, for example, interviewing one for a term paper or other school project. Or you may simply tell a doctor you know that you are interested in his or her profession and request an information interview. Come to the interview prepared to ask questions. Ask the doctor how he or she got started in the field. What does he or she like most about the job, and what least? What were the years of school like? People are often happy to talk about their jobs if you show a sincere interest, and you may even discover a mentor in this way.

As in any career, reading as much as possible about the profession, talking with a high school counselor, and interviewing those working in the field are other important ways to explore your interest.

You can also visit Tomorrow's Doctors (http://www.aamc.org/students/start.htm), a Web site created by the Association of American Medical Colleges to help educate students about the field.

EMPLOYERS

Physicians can find employment in a wide variety of settings, including hospitals, nursing homes, managed care offices, prisons, schools and universities, research laboratories, trauma centers, clinics, and public health centers. Some are self-employed in their own or group practices. In the past, many physicians went into business for themselves, either by starting their own practice or by becoming a partner in an existing one. Few physicians—about 12 percent—are choosing to follow this path today. There are a number of reasons for this shift. Often, the costs of starting a practice or buying into an existing practice are too high. Most are choosing to take salaried positions with hospitals or groups of physicians.

Jobs for physicians are available all over the world, although licensing requirements may vary. In less developed countries, there is great demand for medical professionals of all types. Conditions, supplies, and equipment may be poor and pay is minimal, but there are great rewards in terms of experience. Many doctors fulfill part or all of their residency requirements by practicing in other countries.

Physicians interested in teaching may find employment at medical schools or university hospitals. There are also positions available in government agencies such as the Centers for Disease Control, the National Institutes of Health, and the Food and Drug Administration.

Pharmaceutical companies and chemical companies hire physicians to research and develop new drugs, instruments, and procedures.

STARTING OUT

There are no shortcuts to entering the medical profession. Requirements are an M.D. or D.O. degree, a licensing examination, a one- or two-year internship, and a period of residency that may extend as long as five years (and seven years if they are pursuing board certification in a specialty).

Upon completing this program, which may take up to 15 years, physicians are then ready to enter practice. They may choose to open a solo private practice, enter a partnership practice, enter a group practice, or take a salaried job with a managed care facility or hospital. Salaried positions are also available with federal and state agencies, the military, including the Department of Veterans Affairs, and private companies. Teaching and research jobs are usually obtained after other experience is acquired.

Most M.D.s and D.O.s practice in urban areas near hospitals and universities.

ADVANCEMENT

Physicians who work in a managed care setting or for a large group or corporation can advance by opening a private practice. The average physician in private practice does not advance in the accustomed sense of the word. Their progress consists of advancing in skill and understanding, in numbers of patients, and in income. They may be made a fellow in a professional specialty or elected to an important office in the American Medical Association or American Osteopathic Association. Teaching and research positions may also increase a physician's status.

Some physicians may become directors of a laboratory, managed care facility, hospital department, or medical school program. Some may move into hospital administration positions.

A physician can achieve recognition by conducting research in new medicines, treatments, and cures, and publishing his or her findings in medical journals. Participation in professional organizations can also bring prestige.

A physician can advance by pursuing further education in a subspecialty or a second field such as biochemistry or microbiology.

EARNINGS

Physicians have among the highest average earnings of any occupational group. The level of income for any individual physician depends on a number of factors, such as region of the country, economic status of the patients, and the physician's specialty, skill, experience, professional reputation, and personality. The U.S. Department of Labor (DOL) reports the following mean annual earnings for physicians by specialty in 2009: general surgeons, $219,770; anesthesiologists, $211,750; obstetricians/gynecologists, $204,470; internists, $183,990; and pediatricians, $161,410. Salaries for family medicine practitioners ranged from $82,630 to $193,250 or more in 2009, according to the DOL. Specialists can earn much higher salaries; for example, plastic surgeons can earn more than $411,500 annually, according to Physicians Search, a physician recruitment agency.

In 2009–10, the average first-year medical resident received a stipend of about $47,458 a year, depending on the type of residency, the size of the hospital, and the geographic area. Fifth-year residents earned about $55,570 a year. If the physician enters private practice, earnings during the first year may not be impressive. As the patients increase in number, however, earnings will also increase.

Salaried doctors usually earn fringe benefits such as health and dental insurance, paid vacations, and the opportunity to participate in retirement plans. Self-employed physicians must provide their own benefits.

WORK ENVIRONMENT

The offices and examining rooms of most physicians are well equipped, attractive, well lighted, and well ventilated. There is usually at least one nurse-receptionist on the physician's staff, and there may be several nurses, a laboratory technician, one or more secretaries, a bookkeeper, or receptionist.

Physicians usually see patients by appointments that are scheduled according to individual requirements. They may reserve all mornings for hospital visits and surgery. They may see patients in the office only on certain days of the week.

Physicians spend much of their time at the hospital performing surgery, setting fractures, working in the emergency room, or visiting patients.

Physicians in private practice have the advantages of working independently, but nearly 43 percent of all physicians worked an average of 50 hours or more per week in 2008. Also, they may be called from their homes or offices in times of emergency. Telephone calls may come at any hour of the day or night. It is difficult for physicians to plan leisure-time activities, because their plans may change without notice. One of the advantages of group practice is that members of the group rotate emergency duty.

The areas in most need of physicians are rural hospitals and medical centers. Because the physician is normally working alone, and covering a broad territory, the workday can be quite long with little opportunity for vacation. Because placement in rural communities has become so difficult, some towns are providing scholarship money to students who pledge to work in the community for a number of years.

Physicians in academic medicine or in research have regular hours, work under good physical conditions, and often determine their own workload. Teaching and research physicians alike are usually provided with the best and most modern equipment.

OUTLOOK

The DOL predicts that employment in this field will grow much faster than the average for all occupations through 2018. Population growth, particularly among the elderly, is a factor in the demand for physicians. Another factor contributing to the predicted increase is the widespread availability of medical insurance, through both private plans and public programs. More physicians will also be needed for medical research, public health, rehabilitation, and industrial medicine. New technology will allow physicians to perform more procedures to treat ailments once thought incurable.

Employment opportunities will be good for family practitioners and internists, geriatric and preventive care specialists, as well as general pediatricians. Rural and low-income areas are in need of more physicians, and there is a short supply of general surgeons.

The shift in health care delivery from hospitals to outpatient centers and other nontraditional settings to contain rising costs may mean that more and more physicians will become salaried employees.

There will be considerable competition among newly trained physicians entering practice, particularly in large cities. Physicians willing to locate to inner cities and rural areas—where physicians are scarce—should encounter little difficulty.

FOR MORE INFORMATION

For information on accredited post–M.D. medical training programs in the United States, contact
Accreditation Council for Graduate Medical Education
515 North State Street, Suite 2000
Chicago, IL 60654-4865
Tel: 312-755-5000
http://www.acgme.org

Visit the AAFP Web site to access career information and other resources.
American Academy of Family Physicians (AAFP)
PO Box 11210
Shawnee Mission, KS 66207-1210
Tel: 800-274-2237
E-mail: fp@aafp.org
http://www.aafp.org

To read the Osteopathic Medical College Information Book *and for information on financial aid, visit the Web site of the AACOM.*

American Association of Colleges of Osteopathic Medicine (AACOM)
5550 Friendship Boulevard, Suite 310
Chevy Chase, MD 20815-7231
Tel: 301-968-4100
http://www.aacom.org

For information on board certification, contact
American Board of Medical Specialties
222 North LaSalle Street, Suite 1500
Chicago, IL 60601-1117
Tel: 312-436-2600
http://www.abms.org

For general information on health care careers, contact
American Medical Association
515 North State Street
Chicago, IL 60654-4854
Tel: 800-621-8335
http://www.ama-assn.org

For information on osteopathic medicine, visit the AOA Web site.
American Osteopathic Association (AOA)
142 East Ontario Street
Chicago, IL 60611-2874
Tel: 800-621-1773
http://www.osteopathic.org

For a list of accredited U.S. and Canadian medical schools and other education information, contact
Association of American Medical Colleges
2450 N Street, NW
Washington, DC 20037-1126
Tel: 202-828-0400
http://www.aamc.org

For information on careers and educational paths, visit
Tomorrow's Doctors
http://www.aamc.org/students/start.htm

Podiatrists

QUICK FACTS

School Subjects
Biology
Health

Personal Skills
Helping/teaching
Technical/scientific

Work Environment
Primarily indoors
Primarily multiple locations

Minimum Education Level
Medical degree

Salary Range
$48,770 to $116,250 to
$166,400+

Certification or Licensing
Required for certain
positions (certification)
Required by all states
(licensing)

Outlook
About as fast as the average

DOT
079

GOE
14.04.01

NOC
3123

O*NET-SOC
29-1067.00, 29-1081.00

OVERVIEW

Podiatrists, or *doctors of podiatric medicine*, are specialists in diagnosing and treating disorders and diseases of the foot and lower leg. The most common problems that they treat are bunions, calluses, corns, warts, ingrown toenails, heel spurs, arch problems, and ankle and foot injuries. Podiatrists also treat deformities and infections. A podiatrist may prescribe treatment by medical, surgical, and mechanical or physical means.

The human foot is a complex structure, containing 26 bones plus muscles, nerves, ligaments, and blood vessels. The bones in your feet make up about one-fourth of all the bones in your body. Because of the foot's relation to the rest of the body, it may be the first body part to show signs of serious health conditions, such as diabetes or cardiovascular disease. Podiatrists may detect these problems first, making them an important part of the health care team. There are approximately 12,200 podiatrists employed in the United States.

HISTORY

Doctors who treat feet first began making rounds in larger U.S. cities in the early 1800s. During that century, podiatrists were called chiropodists, after the Greek word *chiropody*. Chiropody refers to the study of the hand and foot. Most other physicians and surgeons of that era ignored the treatment of foot disorders.

The first offices devoted exclusively to foot care were established in 1841. The chiropodists of this period had difficulty competing with physicians in the care of ingrown toenails. The law read that a chiropodist had no right to make incisions involving the structures below the true skin. Treatments included removal of corns, warts, calluses, bunions, abnormal nails, and general foot care.

The term *chiropody* was eventually replaced by *podiatry*, likely because chiropody dealt mainly with the foot.

Modern podiatric medicine emerged in the early 1900s. More recently, surgery has become a necessary part of podiatric care. Today, the skills of podiatric physicians are in increasing demand, because foot disorders are among the most common and most often neglected health problems affecting people in the United States.

THE JOB

Podiatrists see patients who are having problems with their feet. To determine the nature of foot problems, podiatrists talk with patients and visually examine their feet. Sometimes, in order to make diagnoses, podiatrists take X-rays, perform blood tests, or prescribe other diagnostic tests.

Podiatrists treat many common disorders, including corns, calluses, warts, ingrown toenails, and athlete's foot. Bunions, deformed toes, arch problems, and cysts are other examples of common foot disorders treated by podiatrists. Among the relatively uncommon foot disorders treated by podiatrists are infections and ulcers related to diabetes. Podiatrists also treat injuries to the foot and ankle, such as breaks and sprains.

The method of treatment varies considerably depending on the patient's problem. For some patients, podiatrists prescribe physical therapy sessions or give instructions on how to perform certain exercises. For other patients, podiatrists prescribe medications, either to be injected, taken orally, or applied in ointment form.

Some foot disorders, such as ingrown toenails and warts, may require minor surgical procedures. Podiatrists typically perform these kinds of procedures in their offices. Other disorders require more extensive surgery, for which patients may be anesthetized. For this kind of surgery, a podiatrist must use a sterile operating room, usually either in a hospital or an outpatient surgery center.

Another responsibility of podiatrists is to fit patients with corrective orthotic devices, or orthoses, such as braces, custom-made shoes, lifts, and splints. For a patient who needs an orthotic device, a podiatrist makes a plaster cast of the patient's foot, determines the measurements and other characteristics needed to make the device, and sends the information to a manufacturing plant called a brace shop. When the device is complete, the podiatrist fits it to the patient and makes follow-up evaluations to ensure that it fits and functions properly. The podiatrist may also make any modifications or repairs that are needed.

Podiatrists frequently treat patients who have injured their feet or ankles. A podiatrist may wrap, splint, or cast a foot to keep it immobile and allow it to heal. In more complicated cases, podiatrists may perform corrective surgery.

A key responsibility of podiatrists is recognizing serious health disorders that sometimes show up first in the feet. For example, diabetics are prone to foot ulcers and infections because of their poor blood circulation. Symptoms of kidney disease, heart disease, and arthritis also frequently appear first in the feet. A podiatrist must be alert to symptoms of these diseases in his or her patients and refer them to the appropriate doctors and specialists.

Podiatrists provide foot care in private offices, hospitals, ambulatory surgical centers, skilled nursing facilities, and treatment centers or clinics. They also work in the armed forces, government health programs, and on the faculty in health professional schools.

REQUIREMENTS

High School
High school students should take as many courses in biology, zoology, and inorganic and organic chemistry, and as much physics and math as possible to determine whether they have an interest in this field. The profession requires a scientific aptitude, manual dexterity, a good business sense, and an ability to put patients at ease.

Postsecondary Training
A minimum of 90 semester hours of prepodiatry education is required for entrance into a college of podiatric medicine. Over 95 percent of podiatric students have a bachelor's degree. Undergraduate work should include courses in English, chemistry, biology or zoology, physics, and mathematics.

There are eight accredited colleges offering the four-year course leading to a doctor of podiatric medicine (D.P.M.). All colleges of podiatric medicine require the Medical College Admission Test (MCAT) as part of the application procedure.

The first two years in podiatry school are spent in classroom and laboratory work in anatomy, bacteriology, chemistry, pathology, physiology, pharmacology, and other basic sciences. In the final two years, students gain clinical experience in addition to their academic studies.

To practice in a specialty, podiatrists need an additional two to four years of postgraduate education, usually in the form of an office- or hospital-based residency.

Certification or Licensing

There are three subspecialties of podiatric medicine recognized by the American Association of Colleges of Podiatric Medicine: surgery, orthopedics, and primary medicine. Although any licensed podiatrist is considered qualified to address all areas of podiatric medicine, certification as a specialist in one of these three areas requires completion of specialized training. Contact the American Board of Podiatric Orthopedics and Primary Podiatric Medicine and the American Board of Podiatric Surgery for more information on specialty board certifications.

Podiatrists must be licensed in all 50 states, the District of Columbia, and Puerto Rico. A state board examination must be passed to qualify for licensing. Some states allow the exams to be taken during medical podiatric college, from the National Board of Podiatric Examiners, as a substitute for the state boards. Nearly all states require applicants to serve an additional residency of at least one year or participate in other postgraduate training of at least one year.

Other Requirements

The podiatrist must have a capacity to understand and apply scientific findings, the skill to manipulate delicate instruments, and, for those with their own practices, good business skills. Most importantly, they should like all kinds of people and have a sincere desire to help those needing care and attention.

EARNINGS

Podiatrists had median annual earnings of $116,250 in 2009, according to the U.S. Department of Labor. Salaries ranged from less than $48,770 to $166,400 or more annually. Podiatrists who worked in the offices of other health practitioners had annual mean salaries of $133,650 in 2009, while those employed by general medical and surgical hospitals earned $107,790. Podiatrists who work for hospitals, ambulatory surgical centers, and other employers receive benefits such as medical insurance and vacation and sick days. Those

Did You Know?

- The human foot contains 26 bones, 33 joints, 107 ligaments, and 19 muscles.
- The average person takes 8,000 to 10,000 steps a day—which adds up to about 115,000 miles in a lifetime.
- Podiatric physicians receive approximately 60 million visits from people with foot ailments each year.
- About 1,000 applicants apply to podiatry medical schools each year. Approximately 500 to 600 students are accepted annually.
- Forty-nine percent of podiatric medicine graduates are women.

Source: American Association of Colleges of Podiatric Medicine, American Podiatric Medical Association

who are self-employed must provide their own health insurance and retirement programs.

OUTLOOK

Employment for podiatrists is expected to grow about as fast as the average for all careers through 2018, according to the U.S. Department of Labor. Opportunities should be best in group medical practices, clinics, and health networks. Demand for podiatrists' skills is rapidly increasing, as the profession gains recognition as a health care specialty and as foot disorders become more widespread. More people are involved in sports and fitness programs, which can cause foot problems or make existing foot problems more apparent or unbearable. Also, a rapidly growing aging population, many of whom may have neglected their feet, will seek podiatric care. The demand for podiatric services is expected to grow even more as health insurance coverage for such care becomes widespread. Although basic foot care is not ordinarily covered by health insurance, Medicare and private insurance programs frequently cover acute medical and surgical foot services, as well as diagnostic X-rays, fracture casts, and leg braces. Many HMOs and other prepaid plans provide routine foot care as well.

FOR MORE INFORMATION

For information on careers and accredited colleges, contact
American Association of Colleges of Podiatric Medicine
15850 Crabbs Branch Way, Suite 320
Rockville, MD 20855-2677
Tel: 301-948-9760
E-mail: info@aacpm.org
http://www.aacpm.org

For information on board certification, contact
American Board of Podiatric Orthopedics and Primary
    Podiatric Medicine
3812 Sepulveda Boulevard, Suite 530
Torrance, CA 90505-2491
Tel: 310-375-0700
E-mail: admin@abpoppm.org
http://www.abpoppm.org

For information on board certification, contact
American Board of Podiatric Surgery
445 Fillmore Street
San Francisco, CA 94117-3404
Tel: 415-553-7800
E-mail: info@abps.org
http://www.abps.org

For comprehensive information on careers in podiatry, contact
American Podiatric Medical Association
9312 Old Georgetown Road
Bethesda, MD 20814-1621
Tel: 301-581-9200
http://www.apma.org

For information on licensing, contact
National Board of Podiatric Medical Examiners
PO Box 510
Bellefonte, PA 16823-0510
Tel: 814-357-0487
E-mail: NBPMEOfc@aol.com
http://www.nbpme.info

INTERVIEW

Dr. David Yeager is a board certified podiatrist at KSB Hospital in Dixon, Illinois. He has been a podiatrist for six years. Dr. Yeager discussed his career with the editors of Careers in Focus: Physicians.

Q. What made you want to become a podiatrist?

A. I wanted to become a podiatrist after visiting one for a foot issue I had when I was a junior in college. I was already premed, and wanted to go into some field of medicine, but was unsure of what specialty. I was really impressed at the scope of podiatric medicine and all that it had to offer as a profession.

Q. What is one thing young people may not know about a career in podiatry?

A. They may not be aware about the overall job satisfaction. When patients come into our office, they are in pain. More often than not, they leave the office relatively pain free. That is instant satisfaction. Also, a lot of adults don't know what podiatry really is—we do surgery, we work in clinics, we have hospital privileges, and we prescribe medicines.

Q. What is a typical day like on the job?

A. I usually perform two or three surgeries in the morning, then see patients at the clinic during the rest of the day. I see anywhere from 40 to 50 patients a day. I usually work four days a week. If I have patients in the hospital, then I am responsible for making rounds. I work in conjunction with a primary care physician and physicians from other specialties. I also take emergency room calls for any foot- or ankle-related problem. Some patients, especially those who are diabetics, see me on a more frequent basis—to check for ulcerations or neuropathies, which could unfortunately lead to serious complications such as amputations.

Q. What are some of the pros and cons of your job?

A. Pros: I am a physician and with that comes many benefits—I earn a good income and can provide a good lifestyle for my family. I can also make my own hours.

Cons: I am a hospital employee, so there is less autonomy than a podiatrist has in private practice. Another con is definitely a degree of uncertainty in the medical field for all professionals right now.

Q. What are the most important qualities for podiatrists?

A. Personal skills are very important. You must be able to articulate the problem to the patient and make them understand the type of treatment needed. I really think the bond between the physician and patient is paramount—otherwise how could any treatment be done?

Q. Do you have to complete continuing education to stay licensed?

A. Yes, in Illinois we are required to complete 50 hours of continuing medical education every two years. This may vary from state to state. Medical advancements really keep us on our toes.

Q. What is the future employment outlook for podiatrists?

A. It's excellent. As more people in the United States live longer, they are going to unfortunately have foot and ankle problems. There will be great demand in the future for podiatrists in small, areas.

Q. What advice would you give to young people who want to enter the field?

A. I would tell students to take all the basic science classes available in their high school. It's important to become familiar with these subjects so they will have a leg up when they take college-level classes. Also, if they are interested in becoming a podiatrist, they should visit one. Students can contact their state podiatric association to receive information from its mentoring network. They can also contact the American Podiatric Medical Association to find shadowing opportunities with local podiatrists. I can almost guarantee that after a day spent with a podiatrist, those students will also want to get into this field.

Psychiatrists

OVERVIEW

Psychiatrists are physicians who attend to patients' mental, emotional, and behavioral symptoms. They try to help people function better in their daily lives. Different kinds of psychiatrists use different treatment methods depending on their fields. They may explore a patient's beliefs and history. They may prescribe medicine, including tranquilizers, antipsychotics, and antidepressants. If they specialize in treating children, they may use play therapy.

HISTORY

The greatest advances in psychiatric treatment came in the latter part of the 19th century. Emil Kraepelin, a German psychiatrist, made an important contribution when he developed a classification system for mental illnesses that is still used for diagnosis. Sigmund Freud, the famous Viennese psychiatrist, developed techniques for analyzing human behavior that have strongly influenced the practice of modern psychiatry. Freud first lectured in the United States in 1909. Swiss psychiatrist Carl Jung, a former associate of Freud's, revolutionized the field with his theory of a collective unconscious.

Another great change in treatment began in the 1950s with the development of medication that could be used in treating psychiatric problems, such as depression and anxiety.

THE JOB

Psychiatrists are medical doctors (M.D.s) who treat people suffering from mental and emotional illnesses. Problems treated range from being irritable and feeling frustrated to losing touch with reality. Some people, in addition to having a mental illness, may also engage in destructive behavior, such as abusing alcohol or drugs or committing crimes. Others may have physical symptoms that spring from mental or emotional disorders. People with mental illness were once so misunderstood and stigmatized by society that they were kept, chained and shackled, in asylums. Today society recognizes that emotional or mental illnesses need to be diagnosed and treated just like any other medical problem.

Some psychiatrists run general practices, treating patients with a variety of mental disorders. Others may specialize in working with certain types of therapy or kinds of patients, for example, the chronically ill. When meeting a client for the first time, psychiatrists conduct an evaluation of the client. This involves talking with the person about his or her current circumstances and getting a medical history. In some cases, the psychiatrist will give the client a physical examination or order laboratory tests if he or she feels the client's problem may have a physical cause. Next, the psychiatrist decides on a treatment plan for the client. This may involve medications, psychotherapy, or a combination of these.

As medical doctors, psychiatrists can prescribe medication that affects a client's mood or behavior, such as tranquilizers or antidepressants. Scientific advancements in both the understanding of how the human brain functions and the creation of more effective drugs with fewer side effects have helped make medications an important element in the treatment of mental illness. Some psychiatrists will only supervise the medication aspect of a client's treatment and refer the client to another health professional, such as a psychologist, for the psychotherapy aspect of treatment. These psychiatrists often work in private practices and focus on the chemical aspects of a person's illness to find medication to help that client. Other psychiatrists, often those working in hospitals or in small cities and towns, may be the providers of both medication management and psychotherapy.

Psychotherapy, sometimes called *talk therapy*, is perhaps the most well-known type of treatment for mental illness, conjuring images of the patient on the couch while the psychiatrist takes copious notes. Although these elements of talk therapy are sometimes exaggerated in film and on television, the depiction of talk therapy as talking is basically correct. By having the client talk about problems he or she faces, the therapist helps the client uncover and understand the feelings and ideas that form the root of the client's problems and, thus, overcome emotional pain. Talk therapy can be used with individuals, groups, couples, or families.

Another therapy method used by some psychiatrists is *behavior therapy* or *behavior modification therapy*. This therapy focuses on changing a client's behavior and may involve teaching the client to use meditation and relaxation techniques as well as other treatment methods, such as biofeedback, a process in which a person uses electronic monitors to measure the effects that thoughts and feelings have on bodily functions like muscle tension, heart rate, or brain waves. This is done so that the client can learn how to consciously control his or her body through stress reduction.

Free association is a technique in which the client is encouraged to relax and talk freely. The therapist's aim is to help the client uncover troubling subconscious beliefs or conflicts and their causes. Dreams may also be examined for hints about the unconscious mind. Subconscious conflicts are believed to cause neurosis, which is an emotional disorder in which the patient commonly exhibits anxious behavior.

Psychiatrists not only see clients, but may also work with other health care professionals in the course of treatment.

In addition to those working in general psychiatry, there are psychiatrists who specialize in working with certain groups or in certain areas. These specialists include the following.

Child psychiatrists work with youth and usually their parents as well.

At the opposite end of the age scale are *geriatric psychiatrists*, who specialize in working with older individuals.

Industrial psychiatrists are employed by companies to deal with problems that affect employee performance, such as alcoholism or absenteeism.

Forensic psychiatrists work in the field of law. They evaluate defendants and testify on their mental state. They may help determine whether or not defendants understand the charges against them and if they can contribute to their own defense.

Other health professionals who may work with mentally ill people include psychologists, who may see clients but are unable to prescribe medications because they are not physicians, and neurologists, physicians specializing in problems of the nervous system. In some cases, a person's disturbed behavior results from disorders of the nervous system, and *neurologists* diagnose and treat these conditions.

Words to Know

Neurosis: An emotional disorder that arises due to unresolved conflicts, with anxiety often being the main characteristic.

Phobia: An obsessive, persistent, unrealistic fear of an object or situation.

Psychoanalysis: A method of treating mental disorders by bringing unconscious fears and conflicts into the conscious mind.

Psychosis: A major mental disorder, in which the personality is seriously disorganized and contact with reality is impaired.

Psychosomatic: A physical illness caused or aggravated by a mental condition.

Psychotherapy: The treatment of mental disorders by psychological, rather than physical, means.

REQUIREMENTS

High School

Start preparing yourself for college and medical school while you are still in high school. Do this by taking a college preparatory curriculum and concentrating on math and science classes. Biology, chemistry, and physics as well as algebra, geometry, and calculus will all be helpful. You can also start learning about human behavior by taking psychology, sociology, and history classes. In addition, take English classes to develop your communication skills—much of this work involves speaking, listening, and record keeping.

Postsecondary Training

When you are deciding what college to attend, keep in mind that you'll want one with a strong science department, excellent laboratory facilities, and a strong humanities department. You may want to check out the publication *Medical School Admissions Requirements* (http://www.aamc.org/students/applying/msar.htm) by the Association of American Medical Colleges (AAMC) to see what specific college classes you should take in preparation for medical school. Some colleges or universities offer a premed major; other possible majors include chemistry and biology. No matter what your major, though, you can count on taking biology, chemistry, organic chemistry, physics, and psychology classes. Medical schools look for well-rounded individuals, however, so be sure to take other classes in the humanities and social sciences. The AAMC reports that most people apply to medical school after their junior year of college. Most medical schools require the Medical College Admission Test (http://www.aamc.org/students/mcat/start.htm) as part of their application, so you should take this test your junior or even sophomore year.

In medical school, students must complete a four-year program of medical studies and supervised clinical work leading to their M.D. degrees. Students will once again concentrate on studying the sciences during their first two years; in addition, they will learn about taking a person's medical history and how to do an examination. The next two years are devoted to clinical work, which is when students first begin to see patients under supervision.

After receiving an M.D., physicians who plan to specialize in psychiatry must complete a residency. In the first year, they work in several specialties, such as internal medicine and pediatrics. Then they work for three years in a psychiatric hospital or a general hospital's psychiatric ward. Here they learn how to diagnose and treat various mental and emotional disorders or illnesses. Some psychiatrists continue their education beyond this four-year residency. To become a child psychiatrist, for example, a doctor must train for at least three years in general residency and two years in child psychiatry residency. Part of psychiatrists' training involves undergoing therapy themselves.

Psychiatrists can also attend an osteopathic medical program leading to the Doctor of Osteopathic Medicine degree. (See "Osteopathic Physicians" for more information.)

Certification or Licensing
Upon completion of residency training, psychiatrists may seek certification from the American Board of Psychiatry and Neurology (ABPN). To be eligible for certification, qualified applicants must have an unrestricted state license to practice medicine; have the required years of residency training; and must pass both a written and oral examination as administered by the ABPN.

All physicians must be licensed in order to practice medicine. After completing the M.D., graduates must pass the licensing test given by the board of medical examiners for the state in which they want to work.

Other Requirements
To complete the required studies and training, students need outstanding mental ability and perseverance. Psychiatrists must be emotionally stable so they can deal with their patients objectively. Psychiatrists must be perceptive, able to listen well, and able to work

well with others. They must also be dedicated to a lifetime of learning, as new therapeutic techniques and medications are constantly being developed.

EXPLORING

You can easily explore this job by reading as much as you can about the field and the work. To find out what professionals consider worthwhile resources, you may want to read the *Authoritative Guide to Self-Help Resources in Mental Health* by John Norcross, et al (New York: The Guilford Press, 2003). To learn about different types of psychotherapies, you may want to read *Essential Psychotherapies: Theory and Practice*, 2nd edition, edited by Alan Gurman and Stanley Messer (New York: The Guilford Press, 2005). Talk with your counselor or psychology teacher about helping you arrange an information interview with a local psychiatrist. If this is not possible, try to get an information interview with any physician, such as your family doctor, to ask about the medical school experience.

An excellent way to explore this type of work is to do volunteer work in health care settings, such as hospitals, clinics, or nursing homes. While you may not be taking care of people with psychiatric problems, you will be interacting with patients and health care professionals. This experience will benefit you when it's time to apply to medical schools as well as give you a feel for working with the ill.

As a college student, you may be able to find a summer job as a hospital orderly, nurse's aide, or ward clerk.

EMPLOYERS

Approximately half of practicing psychiatrists work in private practice; many others combine private practice with work in a health care institution. These institutions include private hospitals, state mental hospitals, medical schools, community health centers, and government health agencies. Psychiatrists may also work at correctional facilities, for health maintenance organizations, or in nursing homes. They are employed throughout the country.

STARTING OUT

Psychiatrists in residency can find job leads in professional journals and through professional organizations such as the American Psychiatric Association. Many are offered permanent positions with the same institution where they complete their residency.

ADVANCEMENT

Most psychiatrists advance in their careers by enlarging their knowledge and skills, clientele, and earnings. Those who work in hospitals, clinics, and mental health centers may become administrators. Those who teach or concentrate on research may become department heads.

EARNINGS

Psychiatrists' earnings are determined by the kind of practice they have and its location, their experience, and the number of patients they treat. Like other physicians, their average income is among the highest of any occupation.

First-year medical interns earned $47,458 in 2009, according to the Association of American Medical Colleges. Psychiatrists earned median annual salaries of $160,230 in 2009, according to the U.S. Department of Labor (DOL). Salaries for psychiatrists ranged from less than $65,590 to $199,910 or more in 2009, according to the DOL.

Psychiatrists who are employed by health care institutions receive fringe benefits such as health insurance and paid vacation and sick days. Those who are self-employed must provide their own benefits.

WORK ENVIRONMENT

Psychiatrists in private practice set their own schedules and usually work regular hours. They may work some evenings or weekends to see patients who cannot take time off during business hours. Most psychiatrists, however, put in long workdays, averaging 52 hours a week, according to the American Medical Association. Like other physicians, psychiatrists are always on call.

Psychiatrists in private practice typically work in comfortable office settings. Some private psychiatrists also work as hospital staff members, consultants, lecturers, or teachers.

Salaried psychiatrists work in private hospitals, state hospitals, and community mental health centers. They also work for government agencies, such as the U.S. Department of Health and Human Services, the Department of Defense, and the Department of Veterans Affairs. Psychiatrists who work in public facilities often bear heavy workloads. Changes in treatment have reduced the number of patients in hospitals and have increased the number of patients in community health centers.

OUTLOOK

The U.S. Department of Labor predicts that employment for physicians will grow much faster than the average for all careers through 2018. Opportunities for psychiatrists in private practice and salaried positions are good. Demand is great for child psychiatrists, and other specialties are also in short supply, especially in rural areas and public facilities.

A number of factors contribute to this shortage. Growing population and increasing life span add up to more people who need psychiatric care; rising incomes enable more people to afford treatment; and higher educational levels make more people aware of the importance of mental health care. Medical insurance, although it usually limits the amount of mental health care, may provide some coverage.

Psychiatrists are also needed as researchers to explore the causes of mental illness and develop new ways to treat it.

FOR MORE INFORMATION

For information on forensic psychiatry, contact
American Academy of Psychiatry and the Law
One Regency Drive
PO Box 30
Bloomfield, CT 06002-0030
Tel: 860-242-5450
http://www.aapl.org

For information on geriatric psychiatry, contact
American Association for Geriatric Psychiatry
7910 Woodmont Avenue, Suite 1050
Bethesda, MD 20814-3004
Tel: 301-654-7850
E-mail: main@aagponline.org
http://www.aagpgpa.org

For information on board certification, contact
American Board of Psychiatry and Neurology
2150 East Lake Cook Road, Suite 900
Buffalo Grove, IL 60089-1875
Tel: 847-229-6500
http://www.abpn.com

For more information on becoming a doctor as well as current health care news, visit the association's Web site.

American Medical Association
515 North State Street
Chicago, IL 60654-4854
Tel: 800-621-8335
http://www.ama-assn.org

For comprehensive information on careers in psychiatry, contact
American Psychiatric Association
1000 Wilson Boulevard, Suite 1825
Arlington, VA 22209-3901
Tel: 888-357-7924
E-mail: apa@psych.org
http://www.psych.org

To learn more about careers in medicine and how to apply to medical schools, visit the association's Web site.
Association of American Medical Colleges
2450 N Street, NW
Washington, DC 20037-1126
Tel: 202-828-0400
http://www.aamc.org

For information on mental health, and to read the newsletter The Bell, *which contains current information about the field, visit the association's Web site.*
Mental Health America
2000 North Beauregard Street, 6th Floor
Alexandria, VA 22311-1748
Tel: 703-684-7722
http://www.nmha.org

For information on mental health issues, contact
National Institute of Mental Health
Science Writing, Press, and Dissemination Branch
6001 Executive Boulevard, Room 8184, MSC 9663
Bethesda, MD 20892-9663
Tel: 866-615-6464
E-mail: nimhinfo@nih.gov
http://www.nimh.nih.gov

Sports Physicians

OVERVIEW

Sports physicians, also known as *team physicians,* treat patients who have sustained injuries to their musculoskeletal systems during the play or practice of an individual or team sporting event. Sports physicians also do preparticipation tests and physical exams. Some sports physicians create educational programs to help athletes prevent injury. Sports physicians work for schools, universities, hospitals, and private offices; some also travel and treat members of professional sports teams.

HISTORY

The field of sports medicine, and nearly all the careers related to it, owes its foundation to experiments and studies conducted by Aristotle, Leonardo da Vinci, and Etienne Jules Marey. Aristotle's treatise on the gaits of humans and animals established the beginning of biomechanics. In one experiment, he used the sun as a transducer to illustrate how a person, when walking in a straight line, actually throws a shadow that produces not a correspondingly straight line, but a zigzag line. Leonardo da Vinci's forays into the range and type of human motion explored a number of questions, including grade locomotion, wind resistance on the body, the projection of the center of gravity onto a base of support, and stepping and standing studies.

However it was Marey, a French physiologist, who created much more advanced devices to study human motion. In fact, sports medicine and modern cinematography both claim him as the father of their respective fields. Marey built

QUICK FACTS

School Subjects
Biology
Health

Personal Skills
Helping/teaching
Technical/scientific

Work Environment
Indoors and outdoors
Primarily multiple locations

Minimum Education Level
Medical degree

Salary Range
$82,630 to $236,945 to
$540,524+

Certification or Licensing
Required for certain
positions (certification)
Required by all states
(licensing)

Outlook
Much faster than the average

DOT
070

GOE
14.02.01

NOC
3111

O*NET-SOC
29-1062.00, 29-1067.00,
29-1069.11

the first force platform, a device that was able to visualize the forces between the foot and the floor. Californian photographer Eadweard Muybridge's serial photographs of a horse in motion inspired Marey's invention of the chronophotograph. In contrast to Muybridge's consecutive frames, taken by several cameras, Marey's pictures with the chronophotograph superimposed the stages of action onto a single photograph; in essence, giving form to motion. By 1892, Marey had made primitive motion pictures, but his efforts were quickly eclipsed by those of film pioneers Louis and Auguste Lumiere.

Following both World Wars I and II, Marey's and others scientists' experiments with motion would combine with medicine's need to heal and/or completely replace the limbs of war veterans. To provide an amputee with a prosthetic device that would come as close as possible to replicating the movement and functional value of a real limb, scientists and doctors began to work together at understanding the range of motion peculiar to the human body.

Sports can be categorized according to the kinds of movements used. Each individual sport uses a unique combination of basic motions, including walking, running, jumping, kicking, and throwing. These basic motions have all been rigidly defined for scientific study so that injuries related to these motions can be better understood and treated. For example, sports that place heavy demands on one part of an athlete's body may overload that part and produce an injury, such as "tennis elbow" and "swimmer's shoulder." Baseball, on the other hand, is a throwing sport and certain injuries from overuse of the shoulder and elbow are expected. Athletes who play volleyball or golf also use some variation of the throwing motion, and therefore also sustain injuries to their shoulders and elbows.

Today, sports medicine concentrates on the treatment and prevention of injuries sustained while participating in sports. Sports medicine is not a single career but a group of careers that is concerned with the health of the athlete. For its specific purposes, the field of sports medicine defines *athlete* as both the amateur athlete who exercises for health and recreation, and the elite athlete who is involved in sports at the collegiate, Olympic, or professional level. Sports physicians treat people of all ages and abilities, including those with disabilities.

Among the professions in the field of sports medicine are the trainer, physical therapist, physiologist, biomechanical engineer, nutritionist, psychologist, and physician. In addition, the field of sports medicine also encompasses the work of those who conduct research to determine the causes of sports injuries. Discoveries made by researchers in sports medicine have spread from orthopedics to almost every branch of medicine.

Arthroscopic surgery falls into this category. It was developed by orthopedic surgeons to see and operate on skeletal joints without a large open incision. The arthroscope itself is a slender cylinder with a series of lenses that transmit the image from the joint to the eye. The lens system is surrounded by glass fibers designed to transfer light from an external source to the joint. Inserted into the joint through one small, dime- to quarter-sized incision, the arthroscope functions as the surgeon's "eyes" to allow pinpoint accuracy when operating. The surgical elements, themselves, are inserted through other small incisions nearby. In the 1970s, only a few surgeons used the techniques of arthroscopy and did so as an exploratory measure

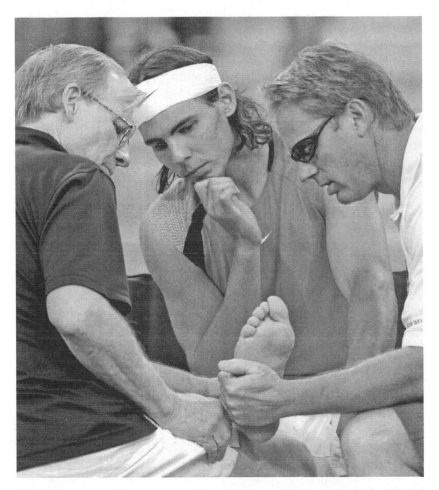

Two sports physicians examine the right foot of tennis star Rafael Nadal after he injured it during a match. *(Kevork Djansezian, AP Photo)*

to determine whether or not traditional surgery had a good chance of succeeding. Today, arthroscopy is the most commonly performed orthopedic surgery performed in the United States; instead of being an exploratory procedure, 80 percent of all arthroscopic surgeries are performed to repair tissue damage.

THE JOB

Sports physicians treat the injuries and illnesses of both the amateur and elite athlete. They are often referred to as team physicians. Depending upon the level of athlete they are treating, sports physicians are usually either practitioners in family practice as *medical doctors (M.D.s)* or *orthopedic surgeons*. More often than not, the individual who works as the team physician for a professional sports team is too busy tending to the health needs of the team to have time for a private practice as well.

At the scholastic level, the team physician is usually the *school physician* and is appointed by the school board. Athletic programs at the collegiate level are usually capable of supporting a staff of one or more physicians who cater to the needs of the athletic teams. The size of the school and athletic program also determines the number of full-time physicians; for example, a state university basketball team might have one physician, even an orthopedic surgeon, dedicated wholly to that team's needs.

Professional teams, of course, have the necessary resources to employee both a full-time physician and an orthopedic surgeon. Generally, their presence is required at all practices and games. Often, professional teams have a sports medicine department to handle the various aspects of treatment, from training to nutrition to mental health. If they don't have their own department, they take advantage of the specialists at university hospitals and private care facilities in the area.

To fully understand the nature of a particular sports injury, sports physicians study the athlete as well as the sport. The musculoskeletal system is a complex organization of muscle segments, each related to the function of others through connecting bones and articulations. Pathological states of the musculoskeletal system are reflected in deficits (weaknesses in key muscle segments) that may actually be quite distant from the site of the injury or trauma. The risk factors for any given sport can be assessed by comparing the performance demands that regularly produce characteristic injuries with the risk factors that might predispose an athlete to injury.

Strength and flexibility, for example, are requirements for nearly every sport. Stronger muscles improve an athlete's performance, and deficits in strength can leave him or her prone to injury. Rehabilitation under the supervision of a sports physician focuses on rebuilding lost muscle strength. Likewise, an athlete who lacks flexibility may subject him- or herself to muscle pulls or strains. For this athlete, rehabilitation would center on warming and stretching the isolated muscles, as well as muscle groups, to reduce or alleviate such muscle strains. In both cases, it is the responsibility of the sports physician to analyze the potential for injury and work with other sports health professionals to prevent it, as well as to treat the injury after it happens. The goal of every sports physician is to keep athletes performing to the best of their ability and to rehabilitate them safely and quickly after they are injured.

To prevent injuries, as well as treat them, sports physicians administer or supervise physical examinations of the athletes under their care to determine the fitness level of each athlete prior to that athlete actively pursuing the sport. During the exams, sports physicians note any physical traits, defects, previous injuries, or weaknesses. They also check the player's maturity, coordination, stamina, balance, strength, and emotional state. The physical examination accomplishes many different goals. To begin with, it quickly establishes the athlete's state of health and allows the sports physician to determine whether that athlete is physically capable of playing his or her sport. On the basis of the physical exam, the sports physician advises the coach on the fitness level of the athlete, which in turn determines a great deal about the athlete's position on the team. Furthermore, the exam alerts the sports physician to signs of injury, both old and new. Old or existing injuries can be noted and put under observation, and weaknesses can be detected early on so that coach and trainers can implement proper conditioning and training patterns.

Depending upon the results of their physical examinations, the sports physician may advise athletes to gain or lose weight, change their eating, drinking, and sleeping habits, or alter their training programs to include more strength or cardiovascular exercises. Routine physical checkups are also a common way of evaluating an athlete's performance level throughout a season, and many sports physicians will administer several exams to gauge the effect of their advice, as well as to ensure that the athlete is making the suggested changes in habits or training.

Preventing injuries is the sports physician's first goal and conditioning is probably the best way to accomplish that goal. Sports physicians are often responsible for developing and supervising the conditioning and training programs that other sports health professionals will implement. The sports physician may work with the coaching staff

On the Web

American Medical Association
   http://www.ama-assn.org
AspiringDocs.org
   http://www.aspiringdocs.org
Careers in Health Care
   http://www.ama-assn.org/ama/pub/education-careers/
   careers-health-care.shtml
ExploreHealthCareers.org
   http://explorehealthcareers.org
How Stuff Works: How Emergency Rooms Work
   http://people.howstuffworks.com/emergency-room.htm
Human Anatomy Online
   http://www.innerbody.com/htm/body.html
Sloan Career Cornerstone Center: Medicine
   http://www.careercornerstone.org/medicine/medicine.htm
The Student Doctor Network
   http://www.studentdoctor.net
Tomorrow's Doctors
   http://www.aamc.org/students
Virtual Family Medicine Interest Group
   http://fmignet.aafp.org

and athletic trainers to help athletes develop strength, cardiovascular fitness, and flexibility, or the sports physician may advise the coaching and training staff members of the overall safety of a practice program. For example, the sports physician may evaluate the drills and practice exercises that a football coach is using on a given day to make certain that the exercises won't exacerbate old injuries or cause new ones. Sports physicians may even be involved in the selection of protective gear and equipment. The degree of their involvement, again, depends on the size of the team and the nature of the physicians' skills or expertise, as well as on the number of other people on the staff. Large, professional teams tend to have equally large staffs on which one person alone is responsible for ordering and maintaining the protective gear.

If a player shows signs of undue fatigue, exhaustion, or injury, the sports physician needs to be there to remove the athlete from the competition. After an athlete is injured, the sports physician must be capable of immediately administering first aid or other procedures. He or she first examines the athlete to determine the gravity and extent of the injury. If the damage is extreme enough (or cannot be determined from a manual and visual exam), the sports physician may send the athlete to the hospital for X-rays or other diagnostic examinations. Later, the team physician may perform surgery or recommend that the athlete undergo treatment or surgery by a specialist.

The sports physician oversees the athlete's recuperation and rehabilitation following an injury, including the nature and timing of physical therapy. Frequent physical examinations allow the physician to judge whether or not the athlete is fit enough to return to full activity. The decision to allow an athlete to compete again following an injury is a responsibility that sports physicians take seriously; whether the athlete is an amateur or an elite professional, the future health and well-being of the athlete is at stake and cannot be risked, even for an important championship game.

Unfortunately, even as research on the field of sports medicine has produced new methods and medications that mask pain and decrease inflammation—which shortens recovery time and lengthens athletic careers—some also produce unnatural performance enhancement. Most notable of these are anabolic steroids—synthetic modifications of the male hormone, testosterone—which have become widely abused by athletes who use them to better their performances. When taken while on a high-protein diet and an intensive exercise regimen, these drugs can increase muscle bulk, which in turn can produce increased strength, speed, and stamina. The side effects of these drugs, however, include aggression, sterility, liver problems, premature closure of the growth plates of the long bones, and in women, male pattern baldness and facial hair. These side effects are usually irreversible and, as such, pose a significant health risk for young athletes.

Another method also banned from use in competition-level athletics is the withdrawal of an athlete's blood several weeks prior to competition. The blood is stored and then, just before the athlete competes, the blood is transfused back into his or her bloodstream. This process (called blood doping) also has serious, even fatal, side effects, including heart failure and death.

Finally, professional athletes sometimes develop substance-abuse problems, such as alcohol or drug abuse. Sports physicians are responsible for detecting all of these problems and helping the athlete return to a healthy lifestyle, which may or may not include competing in their sport.

In addition to the responsibilities and duties outlined above, many sports physicians also perform clinical studies and work with researchers to determine ways of improving sports medicine practices. Often, the results of such studies and research are published in medical journals and popular magazines.

REQUIREMENTS

High School

During high school, take as many health and sports-related classes as possible. Biology, chemistry, health, computers, and English are important core courses. High grades in high school are important for anyone aspiring to join the medical profession, because competition for acceptance into medical programs at colleges and universities is always tough.

Postsecondary Training

Sports physicians have either an M.D. (medical doctor degree) or a D.O. (doctor of osteopathy degree). Each involves completing four years of college, followed by four years of medical school, study and internship at an accredited medical school, and up to six years of residency training in a medical specialty, such as surgery. Many physicians also complete a fellowship in sports medicine either during or after their residency.

During the first two years of medical school, medical students usually spend most of their time in classrooms learning anatomy, physiology, biology, and chemistry, among other subjects. In their last two years, they begin seeing patients in a clinic, observing and working with doctors to treat patients and develop their diagnostic skills. Some medical schools are beginning to alter this time-honored tradition by having medical students begin to work with patients much sooner than two years into their schooling, but this method of combining classroom and clinical experiences is not yet fully accepted or integrated into the curriculum.

After medical school, the new doctors spend a year in an internship program, followed by several years in a residency training program in their area of specialty. Most sports physicians complete this stage of their training by working in orthopedics or general practice.

The fellowship portion of a doctor's training is essential if he or she has chosen to specialize. For example, the doctor specializing in general surgery and interested in sports medicine would probably seek an orthopedics fellowship providing further training in orthopedic surgery techniques.

Certification or Licensing

Sports physicians can become board certified in orthopaedic sports medicine by the American Board of Orthopaedic Surgery. The American Board of Family Medicine also offers certification. Contact the boards for more information on certification requirements.

To become licensed, doctors must have completed postsecondary training in accordance with the guidelines and rules of their chosen area or specialty. Beyond the formal requirements, this usually involves a qualifying written exam, followed by in-depth oral examinations designed to test the candidate's knowledge and expertise.

Other Requirements
To be a successful sports physician, you must be able to learn and remember all the many parts of the human body and how they function together. Knowledge of different sports and their demands on an athlete's body is also important. Like all medical doctors, you need to be able to communicate clearly to your patients with compassion and understanding.

EXPLORING

High school students interested in becoming sports physicians should look into the possibility of working with the physician, coach, or athletic trainer for one of their school's teams. Firsthand experience is the best way to gain fresh perspective into the role of the team physician. Later on, when applying for other paid or volunteer positions, it will help to have already had sports-related experience.

EMPLOYERS

Most sports physicians are in private practice, so they work for themselves or with other medical doctors. Some sports physicians, however, may work for sports clinics, rehabilitation centers, hospitals, and college/university teaching hospitals. Still other sports physicians travel with professional baseball, basketball, football, hockey, and soccer teams to attend to those specific athletes.

STARTING OUT

You won't become the team physician for a National Basketball Association team fresh out of medical school. Many sports physicians begin by joining an existing practice and volunteering with a local sports organization. After several years they may apply to the school board for consideration as a team physician for their local school district. Later, they may apply for a position with a college team until they ultimately seek a position with a national or international professional athletics team or organization. This gradual climb occurs while the individual also pursues a successful private practice and builds a strong, solid reputation. Often, the sports physician's established reputation in an area of specialty draws the attention of coaches and management looking to hire a physician for their team. Others take a more aggressive and ambitious route and immediately begin applying for positions with various professional sports teams as an assistant team physician. As in any other field, contacts can prove to be extremely useful, as are previous experiences in the field. For example, a summer internship during high school or college with a professional hockey team might lead to a job possibility with that hockey team years later. Employment opportunities depend on the skill and ambitions of each job candidate.

ADVANCEMENT

Depending on the nature of an aspiring sports physician's affiliation with athletic organizations (part time or full time), advancement paths will vary. For most sports physicians, advancement will accompany the successful development of their private practices. For those few sports physicians who are employed full time by professional athletic organizations, advancement from assistant to team physician is usually accompanied by increased responsibilities and a corresponding increase in salary.

EARNINGS

The earnings of a sports physician vary depending upon his or her responsibilities and the size and nature of the team. The private sports physician of a professional individual athlete, such as a figure skater or long-distance runner, will most likely earn far less than the team physician for a professional football or basketball team, primarily because the earnings of the team are so much greater so the organization can afford to pay more for the physician's services. On the other hand, the team physician for the professional basketball team probably wouldn't have time for a private practice, although the sports physician for the figure skater or runner would, in all likelihood, also have a private practice or work for a sports health facility.

First-year medical interns earned $47,458 in 2009, according to the Association of American Medical Colleges.

According to the U.S. Department of Labor, general practitioners and family practice physicians earned a mean annual income of approximately $168,550 in 2009. Ten percent of these physicians earned less than $82,630 annually in that same year, and some earned significantly more. Salaries for orthopedic surgeons in practice three years or longer ranged from $237,731 to $540,524, according to Physicians Search, a physician recruitment agency.

Sports medicine physicians, in general, earned less than $172,469 to $307,705 or more, with median annual earnings of $236,945 in 2009, according to a survey by Salary.com. This general figure does not include the fees and other income sports physicians receive from the various athletic organizations for which they work. Again, these fees will vary according to the size of the team, the location, and the level of the athletic organization (high school, college, or professional, being the most common). The income generated from these fees is far less than what they earn in their private practices. On the other hand, those team physicians who are employed full time by a professional organization will likely make more than their nonprofessional sports counterparts, even as much as $1 million or more.

Sports physicians who are salaried employees of sports teams typically receive benefits such as health insurance. Those who are self-employed must provide their own benefits.

WORK ENVIRONMENT

Sports physicians must be ready for a variety of work conditions, from the sterile, well-lighted hospital operating room to the concrete bleachers at an outdoor municipal swimming pool. The work environment is as diverse as the sports in which athletes are involved. Although most of their day-to-day responsibilities will be carried out in clean, comfortable surroundings, on game day sports physicians are expected to be where the athletes are, and that might be a muddy field (football and soccer); a snow-covered forest (cross-country skiing); a hot, dusty track (track and field); or a steamy ring (boxing). Picture the playing field of any given sport and that is where you will find sports physicians. They are also expected to travel with the athletes whenever they go out of town. This means being away from their home and family, often for several days, depending on the nature, level, and location of the competition.

OUTLOOK

After years of watching athletes close down the bars after a game, coaches and management now realize the benefits of good health and nutrition. Within the world of professional sports, the word is out: Proper nutrition, conditioning, and training prevent injuries to athletes, and preventing injuries is the key when those athletes are making their owners revenues in the billions of dollars. A top sports physician, then, is a worthwhile investment for any professional team. Thus, the outlook for sports physicians remains strong.

Even outside the realm of professional sports, amateur athletes require the skills and expertise of talented sports physicians to handle the aches and pains that come from pulling muscles and overtaxing aging knees. Athletes of all ages and abilities take their competitions seriously, and are as prone to injury as any professional athlete, if not more, because amateur athletes in general spend less time conditioning their bodies.

FOR MORE INFORMATION

For information on board certification, contact
American Board of Family Medicine
1648 McGrathiana Parkway, Suite 550
Lexington, KY 40511-1247
Tel: 888-995-5700
E-mail: help@theabfm.org
https://www.theabfm.org

For information on certification, contact
American Board of Orthopaedic Surgery
400 Silver Cedar Court
Chapel Hill, NC 27514-1585
Tel: 919-929-7103
https://www.abos.org

To obtain publications about sports medicine, contact
American College of Sports Medicine
PO Box 1440
Indianapolis, IN 46206-1440
Tel: 317-637-9200
http://www.acsm.org

For general information on sports medicine, contact
American Orthopaedic Society for Sports Medicine
6300 North River Road, Suite 500
Rosemont, IL 60018-4206
Tel: 847-292-4900
E-mail: aossm@aossm.org
http://www.sportsmed.org

Surgeons

OVERVIEW

Surgeons are physicians who make diagnoses and provide preoperative, operative, and postoperative care in surgery affecting almost any part of the body. These doctors also work with trauma victims and the critically ill. Approximately 44,560 surgeons are employed in the United States.

HISTORY

Surgery is perhaps the oldest of all medical specialties. Evidence from ancient Egypt, Greece, China, and India suggests that humans have always performed and worked on developing surgical procedures.

The field of surgery advanced during the 18th century when knowledge of anatomy increased through developments in pathology. At this time, common procedures included amputations as well as tumor and bladder stone removal. Surgery patients were usually tied down or sedated with alcoholic beverages or opium during the procedures.

The late 19th century brought major developments that advanced surgical procedures. Anesthesia was introduced in 1846. Also, Louis Pasteur's understanding of bacteria later resulted in the development of antiseptic by Joseph Lister in 1867. The introduction of anesthesia coupled with the use of antiseptic methods resulted in the new phase of modern surgery.

Surgical advances during the past century include the separation of surgical specialties, the development of surgical tools and X-rays, as well as continued technological advances that create alternatives to traditional procedures, such as laproscopic surgery with lasers.

THE JOB

The work of a surgeon will vary according to his or her work environment and specialty. For example, a general surgeon who specializes in trauma care would most likely work in a large, urban hospital where he or she would spend a great deal of time in the operating room performing emergency surgical procedures at a moment's notice. On the other hand, a general surgeon who specializes in hernia repair would probably have a more predictable work schedule and would spend much of his or her time in an ambulatory (also called outpatient) surgery center.

The surgeon is responsible for the diagnosis of the patient, for performing operations, and for providing patients with postoperative surgical care and treatment. In emergency room situations, the patient typically comes in with an injury or severe pain. If the patient needs surgery, the on-duty general surgeon will schedule the surgery. Depending on the urgency of the case, surgery may be scheduled for the following day, or the patient will be operated on immediately.

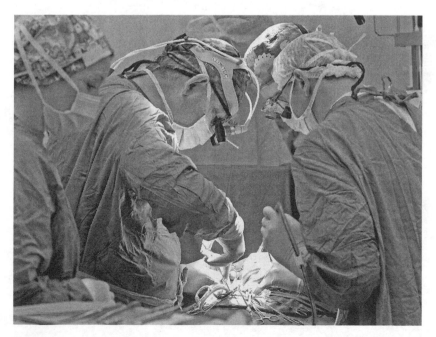

Surgeons perform heart surgery on a patient. *(Novosti/Topham/The Image Works)*

Words to Know

Drape: Sterile cloth used to surround and isolate the actual site or location of the operation on the patient's body.

Endoscope: An instrument used to visually examine the interior of a hollow organ.

Forceps: An instrument that looks like cooking tongs; used by surgeons to hold back skin or other soft tissue.

Scrubbing: The cleaning of the hands, wrists, and forearms of the surgeon and all surgical staff before surgery. This is done to kill germs and harmful bacteria.

Sterile field: The sterile area in which the surgery takes place; any object or person entering this area must be sterilized, or completely free of germs and bacteria.

Suture: The stitches used to close a wound or surgical incision.

A surgeon sees such cases as gunshot, stabbing, and accident victims. Other cases that often involve emergency surgery include appendectomies and removal of kidney stones. When certain problems, such as a kidney stone or inflamed appendix, are diagnosed at an early stage, the surgeon can perform nonemergency surgery.

There are several specialties of surgery and four areas of subspecialization of general surgery. For these areas, the surgeon can receive further education and training leading to certification. A few of these specializations include neurosurgery (care for disorders of the nervous system), plastic and reconstructive surgery (care for defects of the skin and underlying musculoskeletal structure), orthopaedic surgery (care for musculoskeletal disorders that are present at birth or develop later), and thoracic surgery (care for diseases and conditions of the chest). The subspecializations for general surgery are: general vascular surgery, pediatric surgery, hand surgery, and surgical critical care.

REQUIREMENTS
High School
Training to become a surgeon is among the most rigorous of any profession, but the pay is also among the highest. To begin preparing for the demands of college, medical school, and an internship and residency in a hospital, be sure to take as many science and mathematics courses as possible. English, communication, and

psychology classes will help prepare you for the large amount of reporting and interacting with patients and staff that surgeons do on a daily basis.

Postsecondary Training
Many students who want to become a surgeon enroll in premedical programs at a college or university. Premedical students take classes in biology, organic and inorganic chemistry, physics, mathematics, English, and the humanities. Some students who major in other disciplines go on to pursue a medical degree, but they generally have to complete additional course work in math and science. All students must take the standardized Medical College Admission Test (MCAT) and then apply to medical schools to pursue the M.D. degree. Medical school admissions are fiercely competitive, so developing strong study habits, attaining good grades, and pursuing extracurricular activities are all important characteristics for a medical school applicant to have.

Students can also attend an osteopathic medical program leading to the Doctor of Osteopathic Medicine degree. (See "Osteopathic Physicians" for more information.)

Physicians wishing to pursue general surgery must complete a five-year residency in surgery according to the requirements set down by the Accreditation Council for Graduate Medical Education (http://www.acgme.org). Throughout the surgery residency, residents are supervised at all levels of training by assisting on and then performing basic operations, such as the removal of an appendix. As the residency years continue, residents gain responsibility through teaching and supervisory duties. Eventually the residents are allowed to perform complex operations independently.

Subspecialties require from one to three years of additional training.

Certification or Licensing
The American Board of Surgery administers board certification in surgery. The board certifies surgeons in the following fields: surgery (general surgery), vascular surgery, pediatric surgery, surgical critical care, surgery of the hand, and hospice and palliative medicine. Certification is available in a number of surgical specialties, including plastic surgery, colon and rectal surgery, neurological surgery, orthopaedic surgery, and thoracic surgery. The American Board of Medical Specialties and the American Medical Association (AMA) recognizes 24 specialty boards that certify physicians and surgeons.

While certification is a voluntary procedure, it is highly recommended. Most hospitals will not grant privileges to a surgeon without board certification. HMOs and other insurance groups will not make referrals or payments to a surgeon without board certification. Also, insurance companies are not likely to insure a surgeon for malpractice if he or she is not board certified.

To be eligible to apply for certification in surgery, a candidate must have successfully completed medical school and the requisite residency in surgery. Once a candidate's application has been approved, the candidate may take the written examination. After passing the written exam, the candidate may then take the oral exam.

Certification in surgery is valid for 10 years. To obtain recertification, surgeons must apply to the American Board of Surgery with documentation of their continuing medical education activities and of the operations and procedures they have performed since being certified, and submit to a review by their peers. They must also pass a written exam.

All physicians and surgeons must be licensed by the state in which they work.

Other Requirements

To be a successful surgeon, you should be able to think quickly and act decisively in stressful situations, enjoy helping and working with people, have strong organizational skills, be able to give clear instructions, have good hand-eye coordination, and be able to listen and communicate well.

EXPLORING

If you are interested in becoming a surgeon, pay special attention to the work involved in your science laboratory courses. Obviously, working on a living human being is a much weightier prospect than dissecting a lab sample, but what you learn about basic handling and cleaning of tools, making incisions, and identifying and properly referring to the body's structures will prove invaluable in your future career. Also ask your science teacher or counselor to try to get a surgeon to speak to your biology class, so that he or she can help you understand more of what the job involves.

EMPLOYERS

There are about 44,560 surgeons employed in the United States. About 53 percent of licensed physicians and surgeons in the United States work in offices of physicians and 12 percent are self-employed. Nearly 19 percent work for hospitals, and others work for federal and state government offices, educational services, and outpatient care facilities.

STARTING OUT

Many new surgeons choose to join existing practices instead of attempting to start their own. Establishing a new practice is costly, and it may take time to build a patient base. In a clinic, group practice, or partnership, physicians share the costs for medical equipment and staff salaries, and of establishing a wider patient base.

Surgeons who hope to join an existing practice may find leads through their medical school or residency. During these experiences, they work with many members of the medical community, some of whom may be able to recommend them to appropriate practices.

Another approach would be to check the various medical professional journals, which often run ads for physician positions. Aspiring surgeons can also hire a medical placement agency to assist them in the job search.

Surgeons who hope to work for a managed care organization or government-sponsored clinic should contact the source directly for information on position availability and application procedures.

ADVANCEMENT

Surgeons typically advance by expanding their skill and knowledge, increasing the number of patients they treat, and by increasing their income. They may become fellows in a professional specialty or serve on the board of a medical association. Others achieve recognition by conducting research in new surgical procedures and treatments and publishing their findings in medical journals.

EARNINGS

First-year medical interns earned $47,458 in 2009, according to the Association of American Medical Colleges. According to the U.S. Department of Labor, surgeons in general earned mean annual salaries of $219,770 in 2009. Even the lowest paid 10 percent of surgeons earned incomes of more than $121,830. Incomes may vary by specialty. According to Physicians Search, a physician recruitment firm, surgeons in practice three years or more earn the following average salaries by specialty: cardiovascular, $558,719; neuro, $438,426; vascular, $359,339; orthopedic, $357,224; plastic, $306,047; colon/rectal, $291,199; urology, $285,356; and oral & maxillofacial; $208,340.

Other factors influencing individual incomes include the type and size of practice, the hours worked per week, the geographic location, and the reputation a surgeon has among both patients and fellow professionals.

Benefits for surgeons include vacation and sick time, health, and sometimes dental, insurance, and pension or 401(k) plans.

WORK ENVIRONMENT

Surgeons work in sterile operating rooms that are well equipped, well lighted, and well ventilated. They meet patients and conduct all regular business in clean, well-lit offices. There are usually several nurses, a laboratory technician, one or more secretaries, a bookkeeper, and a receptionist available to assist the surgeon.

General practitioners usually see patients by appointments that are scheduled according to individual requirements. They may reserve all mornings for hospital visits and minor surgery. They may see patients in the office only on certain days of the week. General practitioners may also visit patients in nursing homes, hospices, and home-care settings.

More than 43 percent of surgeons worked 50 or more hours a week in 2008, according to the U.S. Department of Labor.

OUTLOOK

The wide-ranging skills and knowledge of the surgeon will always be in demand, whether or not the surgeon has a subspecialty. According to the *Occupational Outlook Handbook*, physician jobs, including surgeons, are expected to grow much faster than the average for all careers through 2018. Many industry experts are now predicting a shortage of general surgeons in the next decade as more students enter nonsurgical specialties, such as anesthesiology and radiology, which require less intensive training. Because of the growing and aging population, more surgeons will be required to meet medical needs.

FOR MORE INFORMATION

For information on accredited post–M.D. medical training programs in the United States, contact

Accreditation Council for Graduate Medical Education
515 North State Street, Suite 2000
Chicago, IL 60654-4865
Tel: 312-755-5000
http://www.acgme.org

To read the Osteopathic Medical College Information Book *and for information on financial aid, visit the Web site of the AACOM.*
American Association of Colleges of Osteopathic Medicine (AACOM)
5550 Friendship Boulevard, Suite 310
Chevy Chase, MD 20815-7231
Tel: 301-968-4100
http://www.aacom.org

For general information about careers, contact
American Medical Association
515 North State Street
Chicago, IL 60654-4854
Tel: 800-621-8335
http://www.ama-assn.org

For information on osteopathic medicine, visit the AOA Web site.
American Osteopathic Association (AOA)
142 East Ontario Street
Chicago, IL 60611-2874
Tel: 800-621-1773
http://www.osteopathic.org

For career information and a listing of medical schools, contact
Association of American Medical Colleges
2450 N Street, NW
Washington, DC 20037-1126
Tel: 202-828-0400
http://www.aamc.org

For information on women in surgical careers, contact
Association of Women Surgeons
5204 Fairmont Avenue, Suite 208
Downers Grove, IL 60515-5058
Tel: 630-655-0392
E-mail: info@womensurgeons.org
http://www.womensurgeons.org

For career information, contact
Society of Thoracic Surgeons
633 North Saint Clair Street, Suite 2320
Chicago, IL 60611-3658
Tel: 312-202-5800

E-mail: sts@sts.org
http://www.sts.org

For information on surgical specialties, contact the following organizations:

American Academy of Orthopaedic Surgeons
6300 North River Road
Rosemont, IL 60018-4262
Tel: 847-823-7186
http://www.aaos.org

American Association of Neurological Surgeons
5550 Meadowbrook Drive
Rolling Meadows, IL 60008-3845
Tel: 888-566-2267
E-mail: info@aans.org
http://www.aans.org

American Board of Colon and Rectal Surgery
20600 Eureka Road, Suite 600
Taylor, MI 48180-5374
Tel: 734-282-9400
E-mail: admin@abcrs.org
http://www.abcrs.org

American Board of Cosmetic Surgery
http://www.americanboardcosmeticsurgery.org

American Board of Medical Specialties
222 North LaSalle Street, Suite 1500
Chicago, IL 60601-1117
Tel: 312-436-2600
http://www.abms.org

American Board of Neurological Surgery
6550 Fannin Street, Suite 2139
Houston, TX 77030-2718
Tel: 713-441-6015
E-mail: abns@tmhs.org
http://www.abns.org

American Board of Orthopaedic Surgery
400 Silver Cedar Court

Chapel Hill, NC 27514-1585
Tel: 919-929-710
https://www.abos.org

American Board of Plastic Surgery
Seven Penn Center, Suite 400
1635 Market Street
Philadelphia, PA 19103-2204
Tel: 215-587-9322
E-mail: info@abplsurg.org
http://www.abplsurg.org

American Board of Surgery
1617 John F. Kennedy Boulevard, Suite 860
Philadelphia, PA 19103-1847
Tel: 215-568-4000
http://www.absurgery.org

American Society for Aesthetic Plastic Surgery
Tel: 888-272-7711
E-mail: findasurgeon@surgery.org
http://www.surgery.org

Urologists

OVERVIEW

Urologists are physicians who specialize in the treatment of medical and surgical disorders of the adrenal gland and of the genitourinary system. They deal with the diseases of both the male and female urinary tract and of the male reproductive organs.

HISTORY

Medieval "healers" who specialized in the surgical removal of bladder stones could be considered the first urologists, but due to his 1588 documentation of urethra, bladder, and kidney diseases, Francisco Diaz is the recognized founder of modern urology.

Advancements in urology came during the 19th century, when flexible catheters were invented to examine and empty the bladder. In 1877, Max Nitze developed the lighted cytoscope, which is used to view the interior of the bladder. By the 20th century, diseases of the urinary tract could be diagnosed by X-ray.

THE JOB

Technically, urology is a surgical subspecialty, but because of the broad range of clinical problems they treat, urologists also have a working knowledge of internal medicine, pediatrics, gynecology, and other specialties.

Common medical disorders that urologists routinely treat include prostate cancer, testicular cancer, bladder cancer, stone disease, urinary tract infections, urinary incontinence, and impotence. Less common disorders include kidney cancer, renal (kidney) disease, male infertility, genitourinary trauma, and sexually transmitted diseases (including AIDS).

The management and treatment of malignant diseases constitute much of the urologist's practice. Prostate cancer is the most common cancer in men and the second leading cause of cancer deaths in men. If detected early, prostate cancer is treatable, but once it has spread beyond the prostate it is difficult to treat successfully.

Testicular cancer is the leading cause of cancer in young men between the ages of 15 and 34. Major advances in the treatment of this cancer, involving both surgery and chemotherapy, now make it the most curable of all cancers. Bladder cancer occurs most frequently in men age 70 and older, and treatment for it also has a high success rate.

Young and middle-aged adults are primarily affected by stone diseases. Kidney stones, composed of a combination of calcium and either oxalate or phosphate, usually pass through the body with urine. Larger stones, however, can block the flow of urine or irritate the lining of the urinary system as they pass. What has become standard treatment today is called extracorporeal shock wave lithotripsy (ESWL). In ESWL, high-energy shock waves are used to pulverize the stones into small fragments that are carried from the body in the urine. This procedure has replaced invasive, open surgery as the preferred treatment for stone disease.

Urologists also consult on spina bifida cases in children and multiple sclerosis cases in adults, as these diseases involve neuromuscular dysfunctions that affect the kidneys, bladder, and genitourinary systems.

The scope of urology has broadened so much that the American Urological Association has identified the following subspecialties: pediatric urology, male infertility, urologic oncology (cancer), renal transplantation, calculi (urinary tract stones), female urology, and neurourology (voiding disorders, erectile dysfunction or impotence, and other disorders).

REQUIREMENTS

High School
If you are interested in becoming a urologist, take courses in biology, chemistry, physics, and mathematics. Courses in computer science are also recommended. Since colleges and medical schools are looking for individuals with well-rounded backgrounds, you should also take English, foreign languages, and history. Many colleges and universities that have medical schools offer special programs for high school seniors planning to attend medical school.

Postsecondary Training
To become a urologist you must first earn an M.D. degree and become licensed to practice medicine. (For more information, see

the article "Physicians.") Then you must complete a five- or six-year residency in urology, of which the first two years are typically spent in general surgery, followed by three to four years of clinical urology in an approved residency program, with the remaining year spent in general surgery, urology, or other clinical disciplines that are related to urology. Visit the American Urological Association's Web site, http://www.auanet.org, for information on residency programs.

The vast majority of urologists enter clinical practice after completing their residency program. However, fellowships exist in various subspecialties, including pediatrics, infertility, sexual dysfunction, oncology, and transplantation.

Certification or Licensing

Certification requires the successful completion of a qualifying written examination, which must be taken within three years of completing the residency in urology. The subsequent certifying examination, which consists of pathology, uroradiology, and a standardized oral examination, must be taken within five years of the qualifying examination. Certification by the American Board of Urology is for a 10-year period, with recertification required after that time.

At an early point in the residency period, all students are required to pass a medical licensing examination administered by the board of medical examiners in each state. The length of the residency depends on the specialty chosen.

Other Requirements

To be a urologist you must like working with people and have a strong interest in promoting good health through preventive measures such as diet and exercise.

The urologist diagnoses and treats conditions of a very personal nature. Many patients are uncomfortable talking about problems relating to their kidneys, bladder, or genitourinary system. The urologist must show compassion and sensitivity to dispel the patient's fears and put him or her at ease.

Excellent communication skills are essential to patient–physician interactions. You should be able to clearly articulate both the patient's problem and the recommended forms of treatment, including all of the options and their attendant risks and advantages. Because of frequent consultations with other physicians, you also need to develop good working relationships with other medical specialists.

Like all surgeons, you should be in good physical condition; you must remain steady and focused while standing for hours. Urologists who work in hospital trauma units should be prepared for the frenetic pace and tension of split-second decision making.

EARNINGS

First-year medical interns earned $47,458 in 2009, according to the Association of American Medical Colleges. According to the U.S. Department of Labor, the mean annual salary for physicians who specialized in internal medicine was $183,990 in 2009. Salaries for urologists in their first year of practice ranged from $100,000 to $195,000, according to Physicians Search, a physician recruitment agency. Those in practice three years or longer reported earnings of $180,080 to $375,000, with median annual earnings of $285,356.

Urologists who work for hospitals and other employers usually receive benefits such as vacation days, sick leave, health and life insurance, and a savings and pension program. Self-employed urologists must provide their own benefits.

OUTLOOK

According to the *Occupational Outlook Handbook*, employment for physicians is expected to grow much faster than the average for all careers through 2018. Employment prospects for urologists are good. The demographics of American society illustrate that the increase in the aging population will increase demand for services that cater, in large part, to them. With baby boomers aging, the need for qualified urologists will continue to grow.

FOR MORE INFORMATION

For information on certification, contact
American Board of Urology
2216 Ivy Road, Suite 210
Charlottesville, VA 22903-4966
Tel: 434-979-0059
http://www.abu.org

For information on careers, contact
American Urological Association
1000 Corporate Boulevard
Linthicum, MD 21090-2260
Tel: 866-746-4282
E-mail: aua@AUAnet.org
http://www.auanet.org

Index